HEAVENLY HUMOR
FOR ALL GOD'S CHILDREN

HEAVENLY HUMOR
FOR ALL GOD'S CHILDREN

WALTER WAGNER

Fleming H. Revell Company
Old Tappan, New Jersey

Scripture references in this volume are from the
King James Version of the Bible.

Library of Congress Cataloging in Publication Data
Main entry under title:

Heavenly humor for all God's children.

    1. Religion—Anecdotes, facetiae, satire, etc.
I. Wagner, Walter, date
PN6231.R4H4   827'.008'031   75-20456
ISBN 0-8007-0760-5 pbk.

FOR

Iona and Sam Darland

who love God and the sound of God's laughter

CONTENTS

PREFACE

Famed soul-winner Billy Sunday once said, "Of course God has a sense of humor. He made monkeys . . . and some of you folks."

Biblical scholar Dr. Charles Francis Potter declares that the Bible can be read on many levels. One is humor. "In part the Bible is for those who appreciate an amusing situation," Dr. Potter points out.

The Book of Proverbs calls for "a merry heart" which "maketh a cheerful countenance" (15: 13), "a continual feast" (v. 15) and "doeth good like a medicine" (17: 22).

Heavenly Humor is offered with the advice of Proverbs in mind, and it goes without saying that nothing in these pages is meant to be sacrilegious or irreverent.

Says Dr. Alex Campbell, a distinguished Episcopalian clergyman, "The first chapter of Genesis tells us that man was made in the image of God. There is no capacity in the mind and spirit of man that isn't already in the mind of God. The mind of the eternal God has a sense of humor in the sublime degree and it follows naturally that man has always had and will always have a sense of humor."

The genesis of this book occurred in the apartment of Reverend Raymond Hoekstra, while he was living in Glendale, California. Present also were Reverend Doyle Hart, and Dr. Warren Walker, whose Life Guides ministry has inspired millions.

All of us agreed that virtually every religious book, and rightly so, dealt with serious matter. There was also unanimous agreement that there was a place for a humorous religious book. The gathering quickly turned into a "joke party"—with the three ministers reeling off story after story.

Their material was augmented by personal interviews I conducted with scores of clergymen and laymen and letters I sent to more than three hundred ministers of various denominations. More than half responded with anecdotes from their own experiences as well as stories they enjoy telling. Ministers, it should be noted, are the first to tell, appreciate, and laugh at a humorous story.

I herewith acknowledge my debt of gratitude to all those who were generous enough to aid me in mining this collection of nuggets from the golden cornucopia of American religious humor.

No single volume, however, can include all the nuggets. A sequel, therefore, is planned, and readers of this book are invited to share their own favorite humorous religious stories for inclusion in the sequel. Letters may be addressed to me in care of the Fleming H. Revell Company, Old Tappan, New Jersey 07675.

In the meantime, readers are urged to put cares and burdens aside and enjoy this effort to provide "a continual feast" of God's humor.

WALTER WAGNER

HEAVENLY HUMOR
FOR ALL GOD'S CHILDREN

1

"GO YE INTO THE WORLD
AND PREACH THE GOSPEL. . . ."

*Episcopal Bishop Phillips Brooks once said, "If any man be
called to preach, don't stoop to be a king." Yet many a preacher
has learned that he's treading dangerous ground in the pulpit.
Sermons often result in both planned and unplanned humor.*

*As for planned humor, one minister has said, "When I preach I
try to make people laugh. And while their mouths are open, I put
something in for them to chew on."*

As for unplanned humor, it's every minister for himself.

One of Billy Graham's cherished stories concerns the evangelist who
was preaching about the dignity of work. He told the congregation that
they should praise God for the opportunity of laboring for their daily
bread.

"But the Lord has seen to it," he said, "that you don't have to labor
every day. Because of Moses you have Saturday off, and thanks to
Jesus you have Sunday off. Isn't that wonderful?"

"Sure is," said a voice from a rear pew. "Five more Jewish boys like
that and we'd never have to work."

"I wonder how many of you folks would be willing to be really honest
and admit you love sin," the preacher challenged.

"I do," said one man.

Raising his voice in shock, the preacher said, "Do you mean to tell
me you're admitting in front of all these people that you love sin?"

"Oh, no, I thought you said *gin.*"

The minister, concluding his sermon on the evils of drink, said, "If I
had my way I'd gather up all the liquor in the world, haul it in trucks,

and dump it into the nearest river. Now let's bow our heads for our closing hymn." The choir director then led the congregation in singing, "Shall We Gather at the River?"

In the moonshine county of the South, a preacher once said, "If a lot of you fellows are ever going to get right with the Lord you've got to stop making whiskey in the still of the night."

"People who use alcohol," said the minister, "don't have a drinking problem. What they have is a *stopping* problem."

A pastor in Texas gave an extremely eloquent sermon entitled "Winning America to Christ." When a famous evangelist read the text, he sent the minister a telegram, which arrived somewhat garbled: CONGRATULATIONS ON YOUR SERMON ABOUT WINNING AMERICA TO CRIME. I AM WITH YOU AND SUPPORT YOU IN THIS WORTHWHILE GOAL. GOD BLESS YOU.

A known backslider told the minister after church: "Wonderful sermon. Everything you said applies to somebody or other I've known or met."

Pastor Doyle Hart once preached a sermon on Jonah and the whale, which he titled: "You Can't Keep a Good Man Down."
In the course of that message, he was so excited that he got a bit tongue-tied, and one sentence came out, "Jonah went into the welly of the bale."

Pastor Barry Wood also remembers a sermon he preached on Jonah. After the service, a woman said, "I was thrilled with your message."

She turned to her young son and said, "Didn't you enjoy Mr. Wood's sermon about Jonah and the whale?"

"I guess so," the boy said. "But I feel just like that whale. All that preaching's given me a bellyache."

The visiting evangelist had delivered precisely the same sermon for three consecutive weeks, and the church board was a little disconcerted.

One of them told the evangelist, "That's a wonderful sermon, but couldn't you give us a new one?"

"I will—as soon as folks in the church start doing some of the things I've been suggesting in the old one."

In his first sermon, the new preacher at the church in Tennessee railed against gambling on horses.

A deacon told him later, "Folks didn't appreciate that sermon. A lot of horses are raised in this part of the country."

The next week he preached about the evils of smoking.

"Too many folks in these parts grow tobacco. You can't preach about that," the deacon said.

The third week he preached about the evils of drinking whiskey, only to be told by the deacon that there was a large distillery less than a mile from the church where many of the parishioners worked.

The frustrated minister asked, "Well, what in the world *can* I preach about around here?"

"Preach against them heathen witchdoctors. There ain't one of them within a thousand miles of us."

The baby cried without stopping during the first fifteen minutes of the minister's sermon. The mother finally got up and walked into the aisle with her infant.

The minister said, "There's no need for you to leave. Your precious child isn't disturbing me."

"Well," she said, "he's crying because you're disturbing him."

One minister took another view of crying infants. Often disturbed by wailing babies, he entitled a sermon "Don't Trust Anyone Under Thirty Months."

The minister had a habit of placing his written sermon on the pulpit about an hour before church began.

A young practical joker noticed the procedure and one Sunday prior to the service he removed the last page of the sermon.

The minister delivered his message in ringing tones. But his final words were on the last page. So he ended by saying, "And Adam said to Eve . . . there seems to be a leaf missing."

Evangelist Bob Harrington is noted for his rapid-fire delivery in the pulpit. He says, "Folks know I'm telling the truth when I preach because nobody could lie as fast as I go."

A lady who'd never heard him give a sermon called Mrs. Harrington and asked, "When can I hear your husband preach?"

She said, "Come over to the house anytime. He's going from daylight till dark."

In New England, the long-standing custom is for a visiting minister to have room and board provided by a local church family. One Sunday, the lady who was hosting a circuit clergyman prepared a table-buckling breakfast of kippers, steak, ham, bacon, eggs, and pancakes.

The minister, apologizing, said, "I never eat on the morning I preach."

The mother and her eight-year-old son attended the service and after it was over, she asked him, "How did you enjoy the minister's sermon?"

"He should have et," the boy said.

"Does your father ever preach the same sermon twice?" a new member of the congregation asked the young son of the minister.

"He sure does—but he hollers in different places."

At the dinner table, a clergyman was telling his guests about a two-hundred-pound fish he'd almost caught.

His little girl said, "Daddy, is that true, or is it like preaching?"

After the sermon, the small boy asked his father what the minister did the rest of the week.

"A minister is very busy," the father said. "There's much church business to take care of. He has to visit the sick. He must comfort people with problems. And, of course, he has to prepare his sermon for the next Sunday. Talking in public is hard work."

"Listening isn't easy, either," the boy observed.

The service in the church always included a group reading of the Twenty-Third Psalm. One Sunday a first-time visitor to the church was reading along, but was about ten words ahead of everyone else.

At the conclusion of the service, one member asked another, "Who was that lady who was by the still waters while the rest of us were lying down in green pastures?"

As she emerged from the church with her parents, the minister asked the little girl if she'd enjoyed the service.

"The music was okay," she said, "but the commercial was too long."

The minister told his parishioners: "There's a theory around that if people don't smoke, drink, overeat, or engage in extramarital sex, they'll live a lot longer. The trouble is, we won't know for sure until somebody in this congregation tries it."

His sermon completed, the minister was about to begin his closing prayer. Just then, he saw a member of the congregation who was asleep and snoring. Distracted, he asked for "every eye bowed and every head closed."

"I sure enjoyed your sermon," the man said to the evangelist visiting the hamlet-sized community. "Yes, sir, that was the best sermon I ever heard."

A woman standing nearby hadn't been able to hear the conversation but was worried about what the man might have said.

She walked over quickly and told the evangelist, "Pay no attention to him, preacher. He's the village idiot."

A woman with eight children came to Dwight L. Moody one day and announced, "The Lord has called me to preach."

"Yes," he said, "and God's already provided you with a congregation."

One preacher pointed out to his congregation, "Jesus promised His disciples three things: that they would be completely fearless, totally happy, and in constant trouble."

The preacher said that God gave every healthy, thinking Christian not five but seven senses—touch, taste, sight, smell, hearing, horse and common.

The missionary was describing to the packed church his adventures in Africa. "One morning," he was saying, "I left my tent and spotted a leopard."

"I thought they were born that way," a small girl whispered to her mother.

Only one farmer had turned out to hear the preacher.

"Do you think it's worth the trouble to give my sermon?" the preacher asked.

"Well, Reverend, if I put hay in the wagon and go down to the pasture to feed the cows and only one shows up, I feed her."

The preacher's small congregation generally sat in the back pews. This Sunday he was delighted to see a stranger sitting in the front pew.

When the service ended, the minister asked him why he'd sat in the front.

"I'm a bus driver," the stranger explained, "and I came to learn how you get people to move to the rear."

There had been so many bicycle accidents in the neighborhood that the minister decided to devote his sermon to the subject.

"What did you think of the Reverend's talk about bicycle safety?" the mother asked her son after church.

"At last," he said, "I understand what they mean by The Sermon on the Mount."

"Every person in this congregation is going to die some day," the preacher proclaimed.

A man near the pulpit began laughing.

Reddening with anger, the preacher pointed a stern finger at the man and said, "Brother, what's so funny about my saying everyone in this congregation is going to die some day?"

The man replied, still laughing, "I'm not a member of this congregation."

"Today I want to preach about liars," the minister declared. "How many of you have read the sixty-ninth chapter of Matthew?"

More than half the people in the church raised their hands.

"You're the ones I want to talk to," the minister said. "There is no sixty-ninth chapter of Matthew."

The minister came to church unprepared but with an explanation: "As you all know, we lost an hour last night because of the switch to daylight saving time. I don't know which hour you lost, but I lost the hour in which I usually write my sermon."

When heavy rain flooded the homes of several residents in Medford, Oregon, the minister sent his young son down to the basement to check for damage.

"Did the water destroy my files?" the concerned minister asked from the top of the stairs.

"No."

"How about my books?"

"Fine."

"And that special chest where I keep my sermons. Are they wet?"

"No, Dad, they're dry as ever."

A misprint in a Virginia newspaper gave the following account of the minister's sermon, "He called on the congregation to repeat their past sins."

The minister with a large radio audience greeted his listeners, "Good ladies, evening and gentlemen of the audio radiance."

The minister illustrated a point in his sermon by saying that a wise providence knows that some Christians grow best in sunlight and other Christians need the protection of shade.

"It's similar to plants," he explained. "Roses grow best in the sun, but fuchsias must be kept in a shady nook if they're going to grow."

Following the service, a woman told the minister, "You don't know how much your sermon has helped me."

"I'm delighted."

Said the woman, "I never realized before why my fuchsias weren't doing well."

The last words of the Texas pastor's sermon were, "I'll be out of town next Sunday so I've arranged a morning service of singing and praise to the Lord."

The young daughter of a minister was in bed with a cold.
"Mom, can I see Daddy?"
"I'm afraid not, dear. He's writing his sermon."
With unexpected formality, the child said, "Mother! I'm a sick woman and I insist I must see my minister at once!"

The Indian in Arizona heard his first Christan sermon. Asked for his opinion, he said laconically, "Big wind, loud thunder, no rain."

Complimenting her minister on his sermon, the parishioner said, "You'll never know how much your message meant to me. It was like water to a drowning man."

The duration of sermons is a frequent source of anecdote. . . .

The minister knew his sermon had gone on much too long and he apologized to his congregation.
"No need to say you're sorry," a woman responded. "You've done a lot to shorten the winter."

The new, unsophisticated minister was concerned. He told a deacon that he'd noticed that many of the parishioners had colds during his sermon the previous Sunday.

Gently, the deacon said, "As time goes on, Reverend, I'm sure you'll begin to realize all those coughs aren't colds. They're time signals."

The service had been lengthy and the preacher said, "I have only ten minutes for my sermon and I hardly know where to begin."

A voice suggested, "Begin at the ninth."

A minister assured his congregation, "Every blade of grass is a sermon."

The next day, as the minister was mowing his lawn, a member of the congregation passed his house and nodded approvingly. "That's the stuff, Reverend, cut your sermons short."

On their way home from church, the couple were discussing the preacher's message.

The wife said, "It seems to me he didn't put enough fire into his sermon."

The husband replied, "In my opinion he didn't put enough of his sermon into the fire."

A Methodist youngster had brought his Catholic friend to his church for the first time.

The pastor took off his watch and placed it on the pulpit as he began to preach.

"What does that mean?" the Catholic lad asked.

"Not a thing!"

Dr. Warren Walker recalls a sermon he preached in Florida. Carried away, he was running long. While he paused to catch his breath, he overheard an exchange from two men in the front pew.

"Is he through?"

"Yeah, he's through, but he ain't quit."

2

THE HIGH AND THE ALMIGHTY

The lighter side of God and His works has attracted the attention of the famous from all walks of life.

Abraham Lincoln was noted for his ever-present sense of humor, and one of his favorite stories concerned two ladies arguing about which side would win the Civil War.

One said, "The South, because Jefferson Davis is a praying man."

The other pointed out that Lincoln also prayed.

"Yes," retorted the first woman, "but the Lord thinks Abraham is joking."

Williams Jennings Bryan, who ran for the presidency three times and lost three times, had just returned from a trip to Europe. He told the New York customs officer, "I have nothing to declare except my faith in God."

One Sunday Mrs. Calvin Coolidge was ill and couldn't accompany her husband to church. When the president returned, she asked, "What did the minister talk about?"

"Sin," President Coolidge said in his usual terse style.

"What did he say about sin?"

"He was against it."

Eleanor Roosevelt often traveled in behalf of good works and charitable causes. On one occasion she was away from the White House so long that President Roosevelt told a friend he had prayed the night before: "O Lord, please make Eleanor tired."

Lyndon Johnson frightened everyone because of his high-speed driving. Said one comedian, "President Johnson drives to church at 85 miles an hour. Last Sunday LBJ got there three minutes before God did!"

Former Vice-President Spiro Agnew became celebrated for his wild, erratic golf game when in one match he hit *three* spectators.

The next time he played, he said to the others in his foursome, "You know, it's hard for me to concentrate on my swing when the entire gallery is reciting the Lord's Prayer."

President Gerald Ford, who watches his personal funds carefully, decided to make an exception in order for his seventeen-year-old daughter Susan to buy a new dress for a ball in honor of the Washington diplomatic corps. The president gave her a blank check and told her to spend as much as she wished.

Susan appeared at the ball in a lovely red chiffon gown and whispered to her father, "Daddy, it only cost fifty dollars."

The president, smiling, asked orchestra leader Meyer Davis to play "Thank Heaven for Little Girls."

Near the close of his life, Winston Churchill said he was at peace with God. He observed in his inimitable style: "I'm ready to meet my Maker, but whether my Maker is ready to meet me is another matter entirely."

In 1923, George Bernard Shaw visited William Randolph Hearst's enormous Sam Simeon estate in northern California. There were 265,000 acres, a private zoo, three guest houses, a total of 146 rooms, a priceless art collection, and entire rooms shipped from Europe.

After Shaw was given a tour of the grounds and the castle, he commented, "This is the way God would have built it if He'd had the money."

Ernest Hemingway's son Jack is an elder at the Episcopal church in Ketchum, Idaho. Following Sunday services, he usually goes fishing. Says Hemingway: "God has arranged things very nicely, since fishing amounts to a jerk on one end of a line waiting for a jerk on the other."

Baseball pitcher Dizzy Dean was the first to admit that he wasn't an intellectual. On being enshrined in the Baseball Hall of Fame in 1953, he said: "I want to thank the good Lord for giving me a strong right arm, a strong back, and a weak mind."

When he reached his ninety-seventh birthday, John Netherland Heiskell, editor of the *Arkansas Gazette,* was asked why he thought he'd lived so long.

The editor replied: "I attribute it to an oversight by the Lord. And I take pleasure in the knowledge that, when God finally realizes His mistake, He won't be able to correct it retroactively."

When he was dying in the hospital, a nurse asked the late Wilson Mizner, wit and soldier of fortune, if he wanted a minister, a priest, or a rabbi.

"Let's have all three," he said. "I want to hedge my bets."

A minister was finally summoned and he asked Mizner if there was anything he could do.

"Why bother?" Mizner said. "I'll be seeing your Boss in a few minutes."

The Reverend William Sloane Coffin, Jr., the chaplain of Yale University was approached by a sophomore who said, "Sir, you must admit that religion is just a crutch."

"Sure it is," the Reverend agreed, "but who isn't limping?"

One famed evangelist received a letter which said, "My life is dull and purposeless and I am bored with the people I know. If I moved to another state and made a new start would things be different?"

The evangelist's answer: "Pardon the illustration but you can ship a donkey from Maine to California. However, he's still a donkey."

Early in his career, one of George S. Kaufman's plays failed during a tryout in Troy, New York. He explained it thusly in a telegram to his father: LAST SUPPER WITH ORIGINAL CAST WOULDN'T DRAW IN THIS THEATER.

Kaufman once had to cut fifteen minutes out of a script. His producer told him the cast would be upset. "How can I explain it to them?"

"Just say that the author giveth and the author taketh away."

Oscar Levant defined an atheist as a man with no invisible means of support.

Comedian Jackie Vernon says that he stopped being an atheist when he discovered he didn't have any holidays to celebrate.

Television's David Frost says that when an atheist dies he's a man all dressed up with no place to go.

The late radio comedian, Fred Allen, had no illusions about his singing voice. He once said, "The first Sunday I sang in the church choir, two hundred people changed their religion."

According to Johnny Carson, "There may be too many religions in Southern California. I saw a three-car crash on the freeway yesterday. Instead of being angry, the drivers got out and formed a new sect."

George Jessel, who has delivered the eulogy at the funerals of hundreds of friends of all denominations, was the guest of honor at a dinner in New York where bonds for Israel were being sold.

Said Milton Berle, "This is the only time I ever heard George talk without first saying a few words to the widow."

"One of the nicest eulogies I ever heard George Jessel deliver was for one of James Mason's cats," said Jack Benny. "You just wouldn't believe what that cat had done for Israel!"

The late comic Herb Shriner said he was surprised by the birth of his twins. "When the doctor showed me two babies I thought God was giving me my choice."

Rodney Dangerfield, the comedian, says this is an age of bargains. "If it had been this way in biblical times, we'd probably have been offered one commandment free, if we accepted the first ten."

Bob Hope, commenting on the 1974-75 recession, "The last time I visited Wall Street they were building an Ark and a Wailing Wall."

Hope speaks often to religious groups. He said recently: "Here I am talking to the Methodists tonight. Tomorrow it's the Catholics. I'd hate to blow the hereafter on a technicality."

Ozzie Nelson received the following letter from a minister's wife in Philadelphia:

Dear Ozzie, In our church Sunday-school class, the teacher asked, 'Who were the first man and woman?' A small boy answered, 'Ozzie and Harriet.'

The teacher said, "No, it was Adam and Eve."

"That's right," the child said. "I always get those two mixed up."

Introducing Danny Thomas, television host Merv Griffin said: "Danny is so religious that when he comes out please give him a kneeling ovation."

Beverly Hills, California, may be the richest community in America, with local family income much above the national average.

Actress Rosalind Russell, who is a resident of Beverly Hills and attends the Catholic church there, calls the house of worship "Our Lady of the Cadillacs."

Comedy writer Hal Kantor says that the churches and synagogues in Beverly Hills are so liberal that instead of the Ten Commandments they teach the Ten Suggestions.

Pat Boone, another Beverly Hills resident, tells the story about the actor who hailed a cab at Kennedy Airport in New York and asked to be taken to the Church of Christ.

The driver deposited him in front of Saint Patrick's Cathedral.

"This isn't the Church of Christ."

Said the Irish cabbie, "If He's in town, He's in there."

Ken Murray, who has lived in Beverly Hills for more than twenty years, relates the tale of the two senior citizens in their nineties who attended the funeral of a friend.

Afterwards, one said, "It hardly seems worthwhile going home."

Ken Murray also tells the story about a minister visiting a racetrack for the first time, hoping to win enough money to repair his church.

The minister strayed to the paddock where he saw a priest blessing a horse. The minister bet the horse and won.

Prior to the next three races, the priest followed the same procedure. The minister bet on each horse the priest blessed, winning every time.

The minister was now about one thousand dollars ahead, and as he watched the priest blessing a horse before the next race, he decided to wager it all.

The horse dropped dead a few yards out of the starting gate.

"I don't understand," the minister said to the priest, "the first four horses you blessed all won. The fifth horse collapsed and died. Why was that?"

The priest said gently, "Reverend, I'm afraid what you don't understand is the difference between a blessing and the last rites."

Accepting an award for his excellent television program, Bishop Fulton J. Sheen said, "I want to give all the credit to my writers— Matthew, Mark, Luke and John."

Lawrence Welk calls those *X*-rated movies *Sinema.*

Art Linkletter's favorite kid story involved a nine-year-old boy.

Backstage at his "House Party" show, Linkletter was told by the mother of one of the children he was going to interview that she was pregnant.

On the air, Art said to her son, "I understand your mother is about to receive a gift from God. Do you want a sister or a brother?"

The boy answered without qualification, "If it's all the same to Mom, I'd like a Shetland pony."

Archie Bunker, America's lovable bigot, was telling his daughter Gloria that it was a miracle he hadn't been killed when a large packing case fell near him while he was at work.

Archie said, "I heard the voice of God telling me to step aside."

"What kind of a voice does God have?" Gloria inquired.

"He has one of them voices you never forget—like Bing Crosby's."

———————————

On another occasion Archie and Gloria were discussing Women's Liberation.

ARCHIE   The Bible says God made men superior to women.

GLORIA   Maybe God made a mistake.

ARCHIE   Oh, no, little girl. God don't make mistakes. That's how He got to be God.

3

SALVATION, SOUTHERN STYLE

There's always been a singular cast to the celebration of religion in the South, which survives to this day.

"Down here we're in revival all the time," says Reverend Jack Taylor, of the Castle Hills Baptist Church in San Antonio, Texas. "Folks in the South are less inhibited in church, they are responsive to worship. They've been known to utter an *amen* or a *hallelujah*. They don't come to church because they have to; they come because it's fun. There's seldom a cold, formal service in southern churches as there are in some places in the north."

To make his point, the Reverend Taylor cites the example of a southerner who was in New York on business. His first Sunday in town he went to church. As the minister began preaching, the southern gentleman interrupted frequently with fervent *amens*.

The minister, unaccustomed to such interruptions, became disconcerted and lost his place in the text of the sermon he was reading. A deacon noted the minister's discomfort. He walked to the southerner and said, "You're upsetting our minister. You'll have to control yourself."

The southerner nodded his consent. A few moments later, however, he was again caught up in the minister's sermon and again he shouted, "*Amen!*"

The deacon came back and said, "I told you to hush."

"I can't help it," the man from the South said. "I got religion."

"Well, shut up anyway. You didn't get it here."

Standing up in a rural Mississippi church to give her testimony an attractive woman startled the congregation.

"I want to thank the Lord for giving me the spirit of forgiveness," she said. "Mr. Thompson over there, he shot my first husband and I forgave him. And I'd forgive him if he shot the one I have now."

The Church Bell, which is Pastor Taylor's weekly newsletter, tells the story of the farmer who was losing his temper while trying to drive his two mules into the field. As the farmer shouted expletives at the unmoving mules, the minister arrived.

"Good morning, Reverend," the farmer said with relief. "You're just the man I need. Can you tell me how in the world Noah ever got *his* two mules into the Ark?"

"I can trace my people back to the days of the Bible," a Georgia belle boasted.

"I suppose they were in the Ark with Noah," her friend said.

"No, darlin', they had their own boat."

Years ago, Oscar Johnson, a distinguished-looking man, entered his Pullman berth at the train station in Louisville.

The porter came in and said, "Governor, are you comfortable?"

Mr. Johnson said, "I am not a governor."

"Yes, sir," the porter continued, "can I get anything for you, Colonel?"

"I'm not a colonel, either."

"What time do you want me to make your bed, Judge?"

'Great day in the morning. I'm not a judge."

The porter was perplexed. "I just feel in my bones that you're something. What might that be?"

"If you must know, I'm the president of the Southern Baptist Convention."

The porter smiled. "Yes, sir! I knew you was some kind of a face card."

A traveling salesman from the north was passing through Bogalusa, Louisiana, and saw an elaborate funeral cortege in front of a church.

He stopped a passerby and asked, "Who died?"

"Can't rightly say," the stranger said. "I reckon it's the one in the hearse."

Says evangelist Bob Harrington: "I not only believe every word in the Bible is true, I even believe the leather is genuine."

In Georgia, the preacher's sermon was devoted to the commandment, *Thou Shalt Not Steal.*

"The Lord," the preacher said, "meant that you shouldn't steal anything. Not even a watermelon."

A parishioner bolted from his pew.

"Where you headed, brother?" the preacher called.

"I just remembered where I left my penknife."

Before the days of Women's Liberation, one southern minister refused to allow women in his congregation to have their own prayer meeting.

Explaining his logic, he said, "If women were allowed to pray alone, there's no tellin' what they'd ask for."

The Arkansas farmer was headed to town for the funeral of his fourth wife. He stopped by his neighbor's place and asked him to attend church with him.

"Wouldn't be right," the neighbor said.

"Why not?"

"To tell you the truth, I'd feel ashamed. You've been right hospitable. You've asked me four times now, and I've never asked you once."

In 1925, the same year of the famed Monkey Trial, the North Carolina legislature considered and rejected a bill to forbid teaching Darwinism or "any other evolutionary hypothesis that links man in blood relationship with any lower form of life."

Sam Ervin, later to become a United States Senator, was a member of the legislature and had opposed the bill. He said, "I don't see but one good feature in this thing, and that is that it will gratify the monkeys to know they are absolved from all responsibility for the conduct of the human race."

Recalling his days as a preacher at a Pentecostal church in Van Buren, Arkansas, Pastor Doyle Hart tells about the young evangelist who got carried away during his sermon. He was preaching on the last days and the imminent return of Jesus. In his fervor, he became one with Jesus, crying, "I'm coming! I'm coming! I'm coming!"

Suddenly the evangelist fell from the platform and landed in a woman's lap.

"I'm so sorry, please forgive me," he said.

The woman answered, "Son, you don't owe me an apology. You warned me three times you were coming and I didn't have sense enough to get out of your way."

The minister in Birmingham, Alabama, was giving a sermon on the lesson to be learned from the experience of Shadrach, Meshach, and Abednego. However, he was a little absent-minded, so he put the names of Shadrach, Meshach and Abednego on a piece of paper and placed it in the breast pocket of his jacket.

"These three boys loved God and they were willing to go into the fiery furnace rather than renounce the Lord. Do you know their names?" (No one did.) "Well, I'm going to tell you."

The minister, in his excitement glanced at his breast pocket, and said, "Their names are Hart, Schaffner, and Marx."

The two small farm boys in South Carolina had been taught by their parents that prayer was important, no matter what the circumstances.

One day the youngsters found themselves in an open field with a bull rushing toward them. Their backs to the charging bull, the boys ran. Glancing back, one of the boys could see the bull gaining on them. He prayed, "Lord, we thank you for what we are about to receive."

The ten-year-old boy was walking with his parents on Elm Street in downtown Dallas. Spying a movie theater, the youngster ran off.

His frantic mother found him inside the theater thirty minutes later. Outside, she said, "Whatever possessed you to go in that place? You know our pastor teaches it's wrong to go to movies."

"Mama," he said. "I just couldn't help myself. I smelled that popcorn, and it smelled so good that I had to buy some. And then the floor of that movie house was so slick I just slid inside."

The young Bible student was witnessing in a suburb of Atlanta. As he approached one house, there was an elderly gentleman sitting on the porch.

"Are you a Christian?"

"No, I'm a Smith. The Christians live two doors down."

"You don't understand. I mean, are you lost?"

"No, sonny. I'm not lost. I've lived here for twenty-five years."

"But are you ready for Judgment Day?"

"When's it going to be?"

"Well, it could be today or it could be tomorrow."

"Don't tell my wife. She'll want to go both days."

The great American pulpiteer, R. G. Lee of Memphis, told the story about a revival where a teenager decided to play a practical joke on the congregation. He went to a costume shop and bought a devil's costume.

He appeared at the revival in his red suit and carrying a pitchfork.

He said to one little old lady, "I'm here to get you!"

Terrified, the woman said, "Mr. Devil. Please leave me alone. I've been going to church for sixty years, but I've been on your side all the time."

At an outdoor Billy Graham Crusade in Dallas, the crowd was disappointing because of a heavy rain.

Mr. Graham was up to the occasion. "There was some talk about canceling the service because of the heavy downpour. But I knew if no one else came, the Baptists would. They're used to water."

Then there was the little southern girl who prayed: "God bless mommy and daddy and my bird and my dog. Take care of yourself, God, because we're going to be out of touch for a while. Daddy has a new job and tomorrow we're moving to Chicago."

4
THE HALO BUTTON

Pastor Barry Wood, of the First Baptist Church in Beverly Hills, observes that whenever a minister makes a house call youngsters press what he calls "the halo button." Immediately, they are on their best behavior or a reasonable facsimile thereof.

As an example, he tells the story of the mother who invited the minister to dinner. But she was worried because her two young sons had picked up the habit of using swear words.

"Tell you what," the mother said, "if you boys don't swear once, I'll give you an apple pie. If you do swear, I'll give the pie to the minister."

The meal was uneventful.

Before the minister left, he said to the boys, "Remember, by God we live and by God we die."

One of the boys chirped, "And yes, by God, you lost your apple pie."

The small girl had been unusually quiet. So her mother went to her daughter's room and was delighted to see her busily at work at her desk drawing a portrait.

"Who's that?" the mother asked.

"God."

"But, darling, nobody knows what God looks like."

"They will when I'm finished."

The letter from an eight-year-old girl to Billy Graham said, "I read the Bible all the time. Adam was the first man and Eve was the first woman. The angel Gabriel was sent by God to Galilee. Jesus prayed for everyone's sins. I know a lot more but I don't want to waste all my paper."

The boy bounced into the house excitedly and told his mother, "There's a lion in the backyard!"

The mother peeked through the kitchen window. All she saw was a stray dog, a large Shepherd.

"Son, you're lying. You go to your room and tell God that what you saw was a dog, not a lion."

The boy went upstairs and was gone for several minutes.

When he came down, his mother asked, "Did you tell God about that lie?"

"Yes, ma'm."

"What did God say?"

"He said the first time He saw that dog He thought it was a lion, too."

The seven-year-old girl was very afraid of the dark. One night her mother asked her to fetch the broom from the back porch.

"I can't because the dark frightens me."

"Honey, Jesus is out there, so there's nothing to be frightened of. Don't you know that Jesus is everywhere? He'll protect you."

"Are you sure Jesus is out there?" the girl asked, gaining courage.

"Of course I'm sure."

The girl opened the door a crack and said, "Jesus, would You please hand me the broom?"

The Baptist boy suggested to the little Methodist girl who lived next door that they play church.

"I'll have to ask my mother," the girl said.

She was back a moment later shaking her head. "Mother says we can't play church because we belong to different abominations."

The backwoods preacher found a small boy all alone, playing in the dirt.

"Where's your father?"

"He was hanged last week."

"Where's your mother?"

"She run off."

"Where's your sister?"

"In jail."

"Is there anybody else in your family?"

"Yup, I've got a brother."

"Where is he?"

"At Harvard University."

"Well, at least one member of your family is doing well. What's he studying?"

"Nothin'. They're studying him."

The occasion was an important one for the six-year-old girl—her parents were going to permit her to attend adult church services for the first time.

Her eight-year-old brother warned her: "Remember, they don't allow you to talk in church."

"Who doesn't allow you?"

"The hushers."

The small boy was spanked by his father for not keeping his room clean.

Tears in his eyes, the boy ran to his mother, saying, "Mom, you should have married Jesus. *He* loves little children."

The father had tried for more than a year to convince his teenage sons to cut their long hair.

On his birthday the father was surprised as he opened a gift box from his sons filled with their sheared locks. The card read: DEAR DAD, FORGIVE US OUR PAST TRESSES.

The minister was proud and grateful that his new church had finally been built. It was so new that the concrete on the sidewalk was still wet.

A little boy, accompanied by his mother, passed by. The boy stepped into the concrete.

The minister lost his temper and bawled the youngster out.

The boy's mother said, "A man of God is supposed to love children, no matter what they do."

"This is one occasion when I can love children in the abstract but not in the concrete."

———

A minister had just received an honorary doctorate from a Bible college.

A friend called to congratulate him and the minister's daughter answered the phone.

"Is the doctor in?" the called asked.

"Yes, but he's not the kind of doctor who'll do you any good."

———

Reverend Jack Taylor passes on the story about the youngster in his church who complained to him about his God-fearing mother, who was a bit of hypochondriac.

"Germs and Jesus," the boy said. "Germs and Jesus. That's all I ever hear about and I haven't seen either one."

———

At a birthday party for a six-year-old girl, one of the guests, a minister, asked her: "What age would you like to be?"

"Seventeen."

"Why?"

"Cause then you're an old woman and pretty soon you'll be with God."

———

Asked what she had learned in her macrame class, the young girl replied, "Thou Shalt Knot."

———

"Is it true, Mother, that we came from dust and that we return to dust?"

"Yes, dear, that's what the Bible says."

"Well," the cherubic child said, "I just looked under my bed and somebody's either coming or going."

The young boy had misbehaved and as his mother was about to give him a tongue-lashing, he said, "I'd like to talk to God."

"Why? Have you done something else that you're ashamed to tell me about?"

"Oh, no, but you'll yell and yell and God will listen, forgive me, and forget about it."

An elderly Congressman in Washington liked to take a nap when he got home. One evening he instructed his grandson to tell anyone who phoned that he wasn't there.

The boy, an avid young Christian, was reluctant to tell a fib. But his grandfather insisted.

The phone rang half an hour later. The boy answered and told the caller his little white lie.

The woman on the other end of the phone sensed the youngster wasn't telling the truth. "I think your grandfather is home," she said. "You'd better go tell him that President Ford wants to speak with him."

Terrified, he ran into his grandfather's bedroom. "Grandpa, wake up! Wake up! The president of the United States is calling. I *knew* that lie was going to get us into big trouble."

The small girl was receiving her first Bible instruction from her grandmother. As the days went by, her grandmother read aloud the stories of the Creation, the Flood, and the Battle of Jericho.

"How do you like the Bible so far?" her grandmother asked.

"Oh, I love it. It's so exciting. You never know what God is going to do next."

The nine-year-old girl was walking along the main street of her hometown with her mother. As they passed a church, they heard the bell toll 12 noon. Then it struck 13, 14, 15, 16, 17, and 18.

"Gosh, Mom," she said, "it's never been this late before."

The youngster had disobeyed his mother and displeased his entire family. As punishment his mother made him sit at a separate table in the dining room during dinner. After the meal was finished and his mother, father, two brothers, and a sister were about to rise, the boy said, "Thank You, Lord, for preparing a table before me in the presence of my enemies."

Seventy-thousand schoolchildren, in a nationwide test sponsored by the government's National Assessment of Education Progress, were asked, "Tell what you know about Eve."

Among the answers:

"She was the first lady of the world—I mean, the first girl."

"She lived in the Garden of Eden and had a husband named Adam Smith."

"They named Christmas Eve for her."

The boy bought a Bible for his grandmother as a birthday gift. But he was stymied as to what he should write in the flyleaf. He thought and thought and then remembered how his father, who was a writer, autographed his books.

The boy gave the Bible to his grandmother with the inscription: 'TO GRANDMA. WITH THE COMPLIMENTS OF THE AUTHOR.'

"Do you go to church?" the young girl asked the new neighbor.

"Yes, do you?"

"We're Methodists, and I go every Sunday with my mother."

"Doesn't your daddy go, too?"

"No."

"Isn't he a Methodist?"

"I'm not sure. My mother says he is a Seventh-Day Absentist."

The pastor noticed that the two boys entering the church were wearing Boy Scout uniforms. He asked them, "Have you done your good deed for the day?"

"I did," the first boy replied merrily. "I helped a nice little old lady across the street."

"And did you help the lady, too?" the pastor asked the other boy.

"No."

"Why not?"

"'Cause she didn't want to cross the street."

The two boys were discussing their fathers.

The first said, "My dad's a doctor. I can be sick for nothing."

The second said, "My dad's a minister. I can be good for nothing."

After attending church every Sunday for a year, the young boy told his mother he didn't want to go anymore.

The mother said: "But you go to Jimmy's house. You go to Philip's house. You go to George's house. Don't you think it's only right that once a week you should go to God's house?"

"Well, how would you feel if you were invited to somebody's house and every time you went, the fellow was never there?"

The boy came home from church filled with excitement. "I got a part in the Christmas play," he told his sister.

"Which part?"

"I'm one of the three wise guys."

"Which Bible story do you like best?" the minister asked the young boy.

"The one about the multitude—you know, the multitude that loafs and fishes."

And then there was the halo button pressed by the little girl when she was spotted late one evening by a minister. The girl was alone, carrying a heavy suitcase, and standing on a street corner.

"My goodness," the minister said, "you're out late. Where are you going?"

"I'm running away from home."

"Do you live around here?"

"Down the street."

"Well, I can see you haven't gotten very far. Maybe I'd better take you back to your parents. They'll be worried."

"I guess so," the girl sighed. "I've been having an awful time, because I'm not allowed to cross the street."

5

SUNDAY-SCHOOL SCHOLARS

The Gospel as rendered by the young has grayed the hair and engendered smiles from Sunday-school teachers, ministers, and parents. Anything can and usually does happen as a result of the weekly confrontations by small fry with the Good News.

There was, for example, the six-year-old boy who wrote, "My favorite Bible story is the one where the plowshares are turned into Fords."

Revenend James Morrison, of the First Presbyterian Church of Hollywood, gleefully recalls the boy who for a Sunday-school assignment about the nativity drew a picture of a jet plane with four passengers.

Explaining his art work, the boy said, "There's Mary, Joseph, and Jesus."

"Who is the fourth passenger?" the teacher asked.

"Pontius, the pilot."

Another example of art work showed three passengers in a large limousine with shrubbery in the background.

The youngster explained: "That's God driving Adam and Eve out of the Garden of Eden in His Cadillac."

Asked to summarize in a paragraph what will happen upon the return of Jesus, one little girl wrote, "When He comes back, it will bring many people great joy. Some will be reunited with their loved ones in heaven. Others with their husbands."

The assignment was to make religious stickers for the windowpanes of the Sunday-school classroom.

"What did you learn from the work you did today?" the teacher wanted to know.

"That if you get too much water on the stickers they won't stick," one boy said.

———————

Then there was this contribution from a member of the younger set: "Samson used the jawbone of an ass to kill the Filipinos."

———————

"What do we learn from the story of Jonah and the whale?" the teacher asked.

"We learn that people make whales sick," the little girl replied.

———————

"What did you learn in Sunday school today," the mother asked her son.

"That God created the world in eleven days."

"But that's wrong."

"In that case I didn't learn anything."

———————

The story of Noah's Ark and the great deluge emerged as follows from the pen of a young Bible expert: "Many were floundering in the great divulge."

———————

When he returned home after Sunday school, the youngster told his mother that the following week the teacher wanted each pupil to bring something to church for the poor.

The mother scanned her pantry shelves. "You can take these cans of sardines that none of us liked."

The boy's face was skeptical. "But that means the poor people are helping *us!*"

"What are sins of omission?" the teacher inquired of her class.

"Those are sins you ought to have committed and haven't got around to yet," a small girl answered.

The teacher's assignment was a short composition about how each child wished to serve God.

"I want to spend my entire life serving the Lord," one youngster wrote. "If I can't have this wish, then I wish for a color-television set."

TEACHER   Why did God make man before woman?
PUPIL   Because He didn't want any advice on how to make man.

Mother's Day brought this essay of appreciation from one Sunday-school youngster. The topic was: "What a Mother Means to a Child." He wrote:

A mother is a person who takes care of her kids and gets them their meals, and if she's not there when you get home from school you wouldn't know how to get your dinner and you wouldn't feel like eating it anyhow.

TEACHER   What's "The Last Supper"?
PUPIL   A dessert.

The boy came home after his first day in Sunday school and told his mother the teacher asked him where he was born.

Mother: "You said the hospital, didn't you?"

"Naw. I didn't want to sound like a sissy so I said Yankee Stadium."

A five-year-old was sent to Sunday school with the following note pinned to her jacket: "The opinions expressed by this child concerning God and the Bible may not necessarily be those of her family."

The teacher had spent the hour telling the children about the mercy of Jesus.

"Now," she asked, "who can tell me what must be done before you can obtain forgiveness of sin?"

One boy spoke up immediately. "First, you have to sin."

"Who wrote the first five books of the Bible?" the teacher asked.

When no one answered, she called on a mite of a girl who answered politely, "It wasn't me."

"I cried at Sunday school," the boy reported to his mother after surviving his first session.

"Why did you cry?"

"I looked around the room, and I was the only guy there that I knew!"

Since the church was warm, the teacher asked the tot to remove her winter coat.

"I can't."

"Why not?"

"Because my mother said that only she and God knows where it buttons."

TEACHER   What did Joshua say at the walls of Jericho?

PUPIL   He rode his horse up to them walls and said, "Whoa, Nellie!"

At the start of the class, the teacher complained of a headache.

"Moses had a headache, too," a sympathetic pupil told her.

"Where did you hear that?"

"My father told me. He said God gave Moses two tablets."

When the little girl, who had three brothers, overheard her expectant mother say she wanted another boy, she said, "Boys! Boys! All I ever hear about is boys. Even at Sunday school we sing hims—not hers."

The youngster was asked to explain a halo.

"It's a circle over the head of an angel. The angel always tries to walk carefully so he stays right underneath it. But if he ever loses it, he just takes his credit card and buys a new one."

TEACHER   What does the story of the Good Samaritan teach you?
PUPIL   That when I'm in trouble, someone should help me.

TEACHER   Why do we no longer send up burnt offerings to God?
PUPIL   To cut down air pollution.

"Today we heard a wonderful story in Sunday school," the youngster told his father. "The teacher said the Jews were chased out of Egypt by Egyptian tanks. When they came to the Red Sea, the Jews saw the Egyptian tanks following them. So they built a bridge and went over safely. But when the Egyptians kept coming, they blew it up with an atomic bomb and the Egyptians were destroyed."

"Did the teacher really tell you the story that way?"

"No, but if I told you what he did tell me, you'd never believe it."

The teacher showed the class a painting of Jesus and was careful to point out, "This is an artist's conception of Jesus, since we don't know what He looked like."

Undismayed, one lad said, "Well, it sure looks like Him."

"Who led the children of Israel out of Egypt?" the teacher asked the class.

No one answered. So she called on one boy. "It couldn't have been me. We just moved here this week from Missouri."

The little girls were talking about their progress in Sunday school. "I'm past Original Sin," the first said with pride.

"That's nothing," the second answered with greater pride, "I'm beyond Redemption."

TEACHER   What did the three wise men bring the Christ child?
PUPIL   Gold, Frankenstein, and mermaids.

"Do you believe that story about Lot's wife looking back and turning into a pillar of salt?" a boy asked his pal on the way home from Sunday school.

"Sure," his friend said. "Yesterday my mother looked back and turned into a telephone pole."

TEACHER   In the Old Testament the Jews believed that cleanliness was next to what?
PUPIL   Impossible.

TEACHER   Who in heaven will wear the biggest crown?
PUPIL   The guy that's got the biggest head.

TEACHER   Who was the strongest man in the Bible?
PUPIL   It was either Samson or Superman, I forget which.

The teacher explained that the children of Israel built the temple, the children of Israel crossed the Red Sea, the children of Israel made sacrifices to God.

"Didn't the grownups do anything?" a small boy wondered aloud.

The six-year-old girl was playing with her infant brother after returning from Sunday school.

"When will he start talking?" she asked her mother.

"Babies don't talk until they're two or three years old," her mother said.

"Yes, they do. They did in the Bible."

"Who did?"

"Well, Job, for one. The teacher said this morning that he cursed the day he was born."

At the Episcopal Sunday school, the teacher said that the Bishop was going to pay them a visit the following week.

When he arrived, the teacher said, "Does anyone remember the title of this important man?"

"Pastor?" one youngster offered.

"He was a pastor once but then he was given a promotion. What is he called now?"

"A door monitor?" suggested one little girl.

After Sunday-school class, one boy was lost somewhere in the huge church.

He was paged over the public-address system and was suitably impressed. "Yes, God," he answered. "I'm right here."

The instructor explained that King Solomon was born about 970 B.C. and died about 930 B.C.

"I wonder," said a youngster, "why everybody in the days of the Bible lived backwards."

Time also threw another Sunday-school scholar into a quandry. After his lesson, he explained to his mother: "The teacher told us today that thousands of years ago B.C. and A.D. had a big battle. A.D. won and that's why we've been on A.D. time ever since."

Another youngster enlightened her parents with a shard of biblical history. "In those days, rich people couldn't afford to buy beautiful printed books. The main reason was they weren't invented yet."

Writing her version of the history of Israel, the little girl noted on her paper: "Israel was started a long time ago and has occupied the same location up to the present time, but sometimes under different management."

The Sunday-school class was expecting a visit from the minister the following week and the teacher was rehearsing her charges for the big event.

Young Tommy was told that the minister would ask the class, "Who made you?" Tommy was then to stand up and reply, "God made me."

When the minister arrived he duly asked the question. There was a long, uneasy silence until a little girl raised her hand. "The boy that God made is home sick with the mumps."

"Christians," one young miss informed her teacher in a written exercise, "are only allowed one wife. This is called monotony."

TEACHER   What does the Bible have to say about bigamy?
PUPIL   That no one can serve two masters.

TEACHER   What was the Tower of Babel?
PUPIL   The place where Solomon kept his wives.

TEACHER   What did Noah do?
PUPIL   He took all the married animals on a boat and left the bachelors behind.

The little girl told her mother that when she grew up she wanted to be a Sunday-school teacher.

"That's wonderful. Why did you make that decision?"

"'Cause you only work one day a week."

The story of Adam and Eve has remained open to various interpretations by youngsters.

One girl told her teacher: "First, God created Adam. Then He looked at him and said, 'I think I would do better if I tried again.' So then He created Eve."

Another young theologian said that God threw Adam and Eve out of the Garden of Eden and put them to work.

"What kinds of jobs did He give them?" the teacher asked.

"They had to clean the swimming pool every day."

One boy explained: "After Eve left the Garden of Eden she went to the hospital and had two children named Cain and Mabel."

"What does the story of Adam and Eve teach you?" the teacher asked the class.

"If you're going to do something wrong, don't do it while God is watching," a boy answered.

"The expansion of Christianity," a pupil informed her teacher, "was due to overeating."

The following are answers to a question submitted by this writer to a Sunday-school class at Calvary Temple in Compton, California.

The question: *What do you think God looks like?*

The answers:

A human being with a heart, feet, eyes like fire, and He shampoos his hair everday.

Tall, gray hair, yellow skin, and brown sad eyes just like my puppy's.

He's tall. He looks like my daddy. He wears a jumpsuit on weekends and has a bald head.

I think God has nice eyes. He wears a very pretty robe, and has a Beatle haircut.

He has white hair and His eyes are bloodshot.

An "unexplantable" figure.

Tall, black hair, wears sharp clothes and a heart necklace.

He looks like Billy Graham.

A tall man with pink eyes and blue skin.

A short man with pink hair.

A kind ole man.

Like the stars.

He looks like Jesus, but I'll tell you a secret. I'm not sure, 'cause I've never seen Him.

He looks like whatever you want Him to look like.

He's an old man because of all the years He's been alive.

He is the picture of health.

I think He's an old man with a long, gray beard. And He sits on a throne like a king of all mankind, and drinks all the Dr. Pepper He wants.

6
SIGNS AND OTHER WONDERS

It's often been observed that brevity is the soul of wit, a truism nowhere better illustrated than on the signs outside churches, on Jesus-oriented bumper stickers, in church bulletin notices, and in newspaper headlines above religious stories.

In the brief period when the God-Is-Dead movement received a great deal of publicity, a church in Little Rock, Arkansas, blossomed with a sign that read:

> GOD IS ALIVE AND WELL
> VISITING HOURS EVERY DAY

The sign outside the Memorial Baptist Church, of Tulsa, Oklahoma, advised:

> COME IN AND HELP STOP TRUTH DECAY

In Chicago, the church sign declared:

> SERMON: THIS SUNDAY
> PREGNANCY
> THE BEST STATE OF THE UNION

Outside a Minneapolis church:

> RALPH NADER ISN'T INVESTIGATING US

In the window of a men's clothing store in Harlan, Kentucky:

WE'VE GOT SOMETHING ON EVERY MAN IN TOWN
SO DOES GOD
GO TO CHURCH NEXT SUNDAY

During the government's freeze on wages and prices, a New York church sign proclaimed:

THE WAGES OF SIN ARE NOT FROZEN

Another version appeared outside a Des Moines, Iowa, church:

EVEN IN THIS AGE OF INFLATION,
THE WAGES OF SIN REMAIN THE SAME.

The sign in a Newark, New Jersey, church said:

FREE BIBLES
COME IN AND BROWSE

During the 1974 recession a church in New York's Wall Street put up this notice:

GOD AND SON, INC.
DOING BUSINESS WITH FOLKS LIKE
YOU FOR 2,000 YEARS.

Another Wall Street house of worship put up a sign designed to appeal to the local financial community:

THIS CHURCH IS ONE OF GOD'S
HOLY OWNED SUBSIDIARIES.

In Lincoln, Nebraska:

> IF YOUR TROUBLES ARE DEEP-SEATED
> AND LONG-STANDING, TRY KNEELING.

In Orlando, Florida:

> FLY NOW
> SO YOU WON'T HAVE TO PAY LATER

In Cheyenne, Wyoming:

> START LIVING TO BEAT HELL

During the energy crisis, St. John's Lutheran Church in New Britain, Connecticut, put up this sign at the suggestion of its pastor, Reverend Carl Widiger:

> COME AND WORSHIP THIS SUNDAY
> NO FUEL SHORTAGE IN HELL

The gas shortage also inspired this outside the Cavanaugh Free Will Baptist Church, of Fort Smith, Arkansas:

> THIS SERVICE STATION
> OPEN EVERY SUNDAY
> FILL UPS FREE

At the peak of the Watergate crisis, when many of those who were involved in the scandal were plea-bargaining with government attorneys, a Washington, D. C., church burst forth with this invitation:

GOD GRANTS IMMUNITY, TOO

When the streaking fad was at its zenith, the Park Street Christian Church in Geneva, Ohio, noted:

STREAKERS REPENT!
YOUR END IS IN SIGHT

On the lawn of Emmanuel Episcopal Church in Boston:

PLEASE KEEP THINE DOG OFF THE GRASS

In a Mexican-American church in East Los Angeles the sign read:

ENGLISH AND SPANISH SPOKEN HERE
WE ALSO SPEAK KINDNESS

Outside the Fifth Avenue Presbyterian Church in New York:

LIFE IS FRAGILE
HANDLE WITH PRAYER

A Las Vegas church promised:

GUARANTEED JACKPOT INSIDE

In Watertown, New York:

SATISFACTION GUARANTEED
OR YOUR SINS RETURNED

A Mississippi church sign read:

SITTING AND WISHING WILL NEVER IMPROVE YOUR FATE.
THE LORD PROVIDES THE FISH, BUT YOU HAVE TO DIG THE BAIT.

A Cincinnati church was obviously attuned to a current television commercial:

WE CURE ALL DISEASES
INCLUDING THE HEARTBREAK OF PSORIASIS

The Toluca Lake, California, Community Methodist church suggested:

SEVEN DAYS WITHOUT PRAYER MAKES ONE WEAK

In San Diego, California, the sign said:

WE ONLY WANT ONE LESS SINNER IN THE WORLD
COME IN AND LET US MEET YOU.

In Toledo, Ohio:

READ THE BIBLE FOR FUN AND PROPHET

The sign on a Baptist church in Glendale, California:

LET US TAKE YOU TO OUR LEADER.

In Oklahoma City:

> CAST YOUR BREAD UPON THE WATERS
> AND DISCOVER YOUR ROLL IN LIFE

In Denver, Colorado:

> WE SPECIALIZE IN FAITH LIFTING

The church sign in Phoenix, Arizona, said:

> IF YOU'RE BEHIND ON YOUR PAYMENTS TO GOD,
> LOANS MADE WHILE YOU WAIT

Sign in the prison chapel at San Quentin, California:

> MORE INN-MATES WANTED

In Fort Lauderdale, Florida, where the Barnum and Bailey circus spends its winters, a church sign says:

> INSIDE—THE GREATEST SHOW ON EARTH

A Navy chaplain tacked this up outside his office:

> IF YOU HAVE TROUBLES, COME IN AND TELL US ABOUT THEM.
> IF NOT, COME IN AND TELL US HOW YOU DO IT.

In Providence, Rhode Island:

> FORGET ABOUT CHURCH AND GOD
> AND NO ONE WILL BE THE WISER
> ESPECIALLY YOU

Everything is blessed in the name of God in Hawaii, but there was a delay in consecrating a new highway. Therefore, the following notice was posted:

THIS ROAD NOT YET DEDICATED
PROCEED AT YOUR OWN RISK

In Kansas City:

YOU CAN FLY HIGHER THAN THE MOON
FREE LESSONS EVERY SUNDAY

On a heavily traveled highway leading into Chicago:

ONLY TWO MORE MILES OF CONGESTION
HANG IN THERE UNTIL YOU
REACH THE FIRST BAPTIST CHURCH

In front of a Baptist church in Alexandria, Virginia:

CHURCH PARKING ONLY
VIOLATORS WILL BE BAPTIZED

The sign in front of the Philadelphia church read:

EVERYTHING YOU ALWAYS WANTED TO KNOW
ABOUT THE HEREAFTER
BUT WERE AFRAID TO ASK

In Lansing, Michigan:

THE OPINIONS EXPRESSED BY THE MINISTER
IN THIS CHURCH WERE STOLEN FROM THE BIBLE.

In front of a Santa Fe, New Mexico, church:

ONE GOD
NO DECISIONS.
NO WAITING.

In New York, a huge sign on a football stadium carried this promising juxtaposition:

THIS WEEK—BILLY GRAHAM
NEXT WEEK—THE SAINTS

Less promising was the juxtaposition of a sign in the lobby of a Miami hotel hosting two conventions:

WELCOME
BAPTIST WORLD ALLIANCE
INDEPENDENT ORDER OF ODD FELLOWS

On a huge rock near Parkersburg, West Virginia, is a painted sign that reads:

YOU MUST PAY FOR YOUR SINS.

Underneath it, carefully lettered, is another sign:

IF YOU HAVE ALREADY PAID, PLEASE DISREGARD THIS NOTICE.

A Boston restaurant has this sign in its window:

FREE WHALE DINNER TO ANY MAN WHO CAN PROVE HIS NAME IS JONAH

Nearby, another restaurant that specializes in fish has a sign that says:

IN COD WE TRUST

The neon sign on a restaurant in Albuquerque identifies it as:

THE GARDEN OF EATIN'

A male clothing emporium on Santa Monica Boulevard in Los Angeles calls itself:

AH-MEN

A garden-supply store in Houston, Texas, is named:

YOUR GARDENING ANGEL

There's still many a business establishment with the sign:

IN GOD WE TRUST
ALL OTHERS PAY CASH

A group of senior citizens were protesting higher utility rates outside the Los Angeles office of the Public Utilities Commission. One picket sign declared:

GOD SAID, "LET THERE BE LIGHT."
SOUTHERN CALIFORNIA EDISON SAYS, "ONLY IF THE PRICE IS RIGHT."

During a strike of cemetery workers in Detroit, a picket sign read:

NO ONE LOWERED UNTIL WE ARE RAISED.

In a church cemetery in Alabama, a sign reads:

PERSONS ARE PROHIBITED FROM PICKING FLOWERS
FROM ANY BUT THEIR OWN GRAVES.

Among the proliferation of Jesus bumper stickers the following have been sighted:

GOT THE BLAHS? TAKE JESUS.

THIS IS A GOD SQUAD CAR.

MY GOD IS NOT DEAD! SORRY ABOUT YOURS.

I WILL RETURN. JESUS SAID IT BEFORE GENERAL MACARTHUR.

JESUS CHRIST—HE'S THE REAL THING.

IF YOU'RE ON YOUR WAY TO HEAVEN, HONK YOUR HORN.

IF YOUR GOD IS DEAD TRY MINE . . . JESUS SAVES.

GO TO CHURCH AND MEET JESUS CHRIST SUPERSTAR WITH THE ORIGINAL CAST

IS THERE INTELLIGENT LIFE ON EARTH? ASK JESUS

REPENT. BOYCOTT HELL.

GET IT TOGETHER IN JESUS

GOD'S SPEED DOESN'T KILL.

BE PREPARED. JESUS IS COMING AT ANY MOMENT. DRIVER WILL DISAPPEAR.

DRIVE CAREFULLY. REMEMBER: IT'S NOT ONLY A CAR THAT CAN BE RECALLED BY ITS MAKER.

Church bulletins are becoming a lively source of entertainment.
One minister wrote in his bulletin: "Please remember the old Chinese proverb—he who parks in the minister's space must preach the Sunday sermon."

A column about church finances in the newsletter of All Saint's Episcopal Church of Pasadena, California, is headed: GLAD TITHINGS.

Wrote a Memphis minister in his weekly newsletter: "I will be on vacation for two weeks. In case of emergency, speak directly to God."

Admitting his church didn't have the world's best choir, a pastor wrote the congregation: "Next week in order to avoid embarrassing encores, music lovers are advised to give quickly."

"Reverend William Hastings will preach in our church Sunday morning, after which the church will be closed for needed repairs," said the announcement in the Colorado newsletter.

A Baptist church bulletin carried a brief story about a reorganization of its brotherhood, concluding with the news: "Starting next Monday, the men of the church will reform."

The Washington, D. C., church bulletin gave the details concerning a new employee: "Our church secretary, who recently resigned from her job as a secretary in the Pentagon, has reorganized the pastor's filing system. One file is now marked SACRED and the other TOP SACRED."

A headline in the Muskogee, Oklahoma, *Phoenix* concerning the completion of seminary studies by Reverend Billie F. Fudge said:

FUDGE TO RECEIVE DEGREE IN DIVINITY

When Notre Dame went coed, the Chicago *Daily News* headlined the news:

IT'S OFFICIAL, MEN
NOTRE GOING DAME

A story in the Los Angeles *Times* detailing the twenty-fifth anniversary of a local disc jockey who plays music designed to appeal to teenagers carried the headline:

DICK WHITTINGHILL
THE ROCK OF SAGES

When Reverend John A. Baxter, of the United Presbyterian Church of La Mirada, California, turned to the hobby of beekeeping, the Los Angeles *Times* punned:

BEES ON EARTH
GOOD WILL TO MEN

The classic of them all concerned the purchase by evangelist Rex Humbard of a girdle factory. *Time* magazine's headline:

ROCK OF AGES RESTS ON FIRM FOUNDATION

7

UP THERE, DOWN THERE

Though no question is more important than where eternity will be spent, discussion of heaven and hell is not without its lighter moments.

Bob Harrington, the renowned Chaplain of Bourbon Street, tells the story about the planeload of one hundred Baptists who died in a crash and went to heaven. But Saint Peter felt they were all backsliders and sent them to hell.

A few days later Satan telephoned Saint Peter and said, "You've got to take them back."

"Why?"

"They've been here less than a week and already tithed $100,000 for air conditioning."

"Doctor! Doctor!" the man asked anxiously as he came awake. "Was the surgery a success?"

"I'm not your doctor. I'm Saint Peter."

The hospital patient opened his eyes after an operation and found the blinds of his room drawn.

"Why is it so dark in here, Doctor?" he asked.

"Well," the doctor said, "there's a fire burning across the alley and I didn't want you to wake up and think the operation had been a failure."

The ailing man phoned his doctor for an emergency appointment. The nurse said the doctor couldn't see him for two weeks.

"By that time," he said, "I could be dead and in heaven."

"In that case," the harried nurse replied, "you can always cancel the appointment."

On an airplane flight, the young divinity student was reading his Bible.

The man sitting next to him asked, "Do you believe every word in the Bible?"

"Absolutely!"

"You mean to say you believe that a whale swallowed Jonah?"

"Of course."

"Can you tell me how that could possibly happen."

"When I get to heaven, I'll ask Jonah."

"Suppose Jonah isn't in heaven?"

"Then you'll have to ask him."

When a survivor of the terrible Johnstown flood arrived in heaven, he asked Saint Peter if he could share the story of his horrendous adventure at the next prayer meeting.

"Certainly," Saint Peter said. "But bear in mind that Noah will be in the audience."

A guide was conducting a group of tourists around the Empire State Building in New York.

On the elevator ride to the 102nd floor, a nervous woman asked, "What if these elevator cables should break? Would we go up or down?"

"That," the guide said, "depends entirely on the kind of life you've been leading."

The seven-year-old boy was taking his first ride in a skyscraper elevator with his father.

After they'd shot up forty floors in a few seconds, the frightened boy asked, "Dad, does God know we're coming?"

Saint Peter fulfilled the request of one of his heavenly companions and let him take a glimpse of hades.

The man was surprised. Down below he saw sinners who were drinking champagne, eating caviar, and dancing.

"Why can't we have a party like that up here?"

"For three people?" Saint Peter asked.

Chaplain Ray, of Dallas, Texas, who's conducted his evangelical prison ministry for more than forty years, was leading an inmate in a penitentiary to Christ.

The inmate, a chain-smoker, had one reservation. He asked, "Does the Bible say that if you smoke you can't get to heaven?"

"No," Chaplain Ray said, "but the more you smoke the quicker you'll get there."

Satan was annoyed with the new, swaggering arrival. "You act as if you own this place."

"I do," the man said. "My wife gave it to me all my life."

From his pulpit, the minister told his congregation, "All those who want to go to heaven remain seated and all those who want to join the devil in hell, stand up."

An inebriated man got to his feet, looked around and then said to the preacher, "Looks like you and me are the only ones who are going to make it."

H. L. Mencken, a religious skeptic all his life, once said, "A church is a place in which gentlemen who have never been to heaven brag about it to people who will never get there."

Billy Sunday liked to say: "If there's no hell, a lot of preachers are obtaining money under false pretenses."

One preacher in Texas, taking note of inflation, explained to his flock: "The reason you can't take your money with you to heaven is because it goes before you do."

———————

A minister in Chicago during a church fund-raising drive had another point of view. "Certainly you can't take it with you," he said, "but you can send it on ahead."

———————

Two young boys were talking and one said, "Did you see that movie, *The Exorcist?* It's about the devil."

"There ain't no such thing as the devil," his friend said. "The devil is like Santa Claus. It's your father."

———————

When the wealthy woman entered heaven, Saint Peter gave her a bicycle to ride over the golden streets.

Pedaling along, she saw her maid go by in a Cadillac and her gardener driving a Rolls-Royce.

Very upset, she went to Saint Peter and asked why her maid and gardener had more luxurious transportation than she did.

Saint Peter explained, "The kind of transportation you are assigned in heaven depends on how good a Christian you were on earth."

Two days later she returned to Saint Peter and she was laughing.

"What's so funny?" he asked.

"Yesterday I saw my pastor going by on a pair of roller skates."

———————

A longtime sinner opened the morning newspaper and was amazed to read in the obituary column that he had died. He immediately phoned his best friend.

"Did you see the paper? It says I'm dead."

"Yes, I read that," his friend said, "and I know where you're calling from."

Saint Peter and the devil agreed that each would repair half the wall between heaven and hell.

Saint Peter made his repairs very quickly. But the devil kept delaying.

Impatient, Saint Peter told Satan, "If you don't fix your half of the wall, I'll have to sue you."

"Impossible!" the devil laughed. "Where in heaven are you going to find a lawyer?"

Meathead, Archie Bunker's son-in-law on the "All in the Family" television show, was discussing religion with his intolerant nemesis.

"Archie, what would you do if you got to heaven and you were met by a rabbi?"

"I'd drop dead."

The good Christian had reached his sixty-fifth birthday, and decided that to celebrate he'd present a new image to the world. All his life he'd worn conservative business suits, a black tie, and a white shirt. So he bought a loud plaid suit, a checked tie, and during the next few weeks, he let his beard and mustache grow.

As he was crossing the street one day he was hit by a car and killed.

In heaven, he told Saint Peter, "I was a good husband. I tithed all my life. I've always been a religious man. Why me?"

"To tell you the truth," Saint Peter said, "I didn't recognize you."

"Young man," said the boss, "do you believe in life after death?"

"Yes, sir!"

"Then that makes everything just fine. You're fired."

"For what reason?"

"About an hour after you left yesterday to attend your grandfather's funeral, he stopped by to see you."

A small community in Michigan is actually named *Hell*. The letter-head of the Chamber of Commerce describes it as: A TOWN ON ITS WAY UP.

———————

Saint Peter was showing a freshly arrived group of Methodists around heaven. As they passed one large house, he said, "Please be very quiet."

"Why?" a woman asked.

In a low voice, Saint Peter said, "The Baptists are behind that door, and they don't know anyone else is here."

———————

A worker for a candidate who was running for mayor knocked on a door and asked the householder to please vote for his candidate.

The householder said, "I wouldn't vote for that man if he was Saint Peter himself."

The vote-getter snapped, "If he were Saint Peter you couldn't vote for him anyway because you wouldn't be in his district."

———————

The atheist was in an argument with his religious friend.

"You don't really believe that when you die you'll go up to heaven and fly around with wings. How in the world are you going to get your coat on over those wings?"

"The same way you'll get your trousers on over your tail."

———————

Saint Peter was surprised to see the new arrival. He'd had no advance warning of his coming.

"How did you get here so quickly?" Saint Peter asked.

"Flu."

———————

"How many of you would like to go to heaven?" the minister asked his congregation.

Everybody except one man raised his hand,

"You mean to tell me," the minister said, "you don't want to go to heaven when you die."

"Well, yes, but I thought you were getting a gang together to leave right now."

According to Chaplain Ray, Saint Peter processes applicants to heaven in a unique way. He gives each applicant a piece of chalk and says, "You start climbing that big ladder and every time you reach another rung, you make a chalk mark for each sin you committed."

An hour later, one man was climbing down the ladder. At the bottom, an angel asked, "Didn't you make it?"

"I don't know," the man replied, "I'm just coming down to get more chalk."

In the elevator of a church in Hollywood are two signs. The first says, IN AN EMERGENCY, PRESS THE BUTTON. The second says, IF THE EMERGENCY BUTTON DOESN'T WORK, HAVE A GOOD FLIGHT.

A preacher was playing golf with Moses and Jesus on the heavenly links.

On His first try, Jesus sank a hole in one.

So did Moses.

The preacher said, "Can't we cut out the miracles and play fair?"

The two ministers in heaven were talking about a colleague, who suddenly appeared from nowhere. One of the ministers inadvertently greeted him by saying, "Well, speaking of the devil . . . ."

A woman dreamed that she was talking with her late husband

"Are you happy now?" she asked him.

"Very."

"Happier than you were on earth with me?"

"Yes."

"Tell me, darling, what's it like in heaven?"

"Who said I was in heaven?"

The mother was explaining to her son that it was very important for him to say his prayers. "If you don't say your prayers, you won't go to heaven."

"I don't want to go to heaven," the boy said. "I want to go with you and Daddy."

The button-nosed little girl asked her mother, "What do angels do in heaven?"

"They sing and play harps."

Surprised, she asked, "Don't they have television sets?"

"Do people who lie ever go to heaven?" the small boy asked his father.

"Of course not."

"Gosh, it must be lonesome up there with only God and George Washington."

X Two friends died and went their separate paths.

From down below, one of the men called his pal in heaven.

"All we do around here is wear a red suit and shovel some coal. I work only about an hour a day. What's it like in heaven?"

"Oh," his friend said, "we get up at four o'clock in the morning, gather in the stars, then we haul in the moon and hang out the sun. Then we have to roll the clouds around all day."

"How come you have to work so hard?"

"To tell you the truth, we're a little short of help up here."

The somewhat brash newcomer, who'd been on the miserly side during his earthly life, told Saint Peter at the pearly gates, "You certainly have a soft job. Just sitting around here century after century."

"But you must remember," Saint Peter said, "that in Paradise a million years are but a minute and a million dollars is like a penny."

"If that's the case, I wonder if you'd loan me a penny."

"Certainly," Saint Peter said, "in a minute."

An evangelist was driving his car through New Mexico. He stopped and picked up a young hitchhiker.

"Are you saved, son?"

"No."

"Do you realize that you're headed for a place filled with sinners?"

"I guess so."

"And only the wicked dwell there?"

The young man nodded his head.

"And do you know what that place you're going to is called?"

"Sure do. Albuquerque."

The minister told one of the backsliders in his church, "I want you to go outside and look up to heaven. You'll receive a revelation."

"But it's pouring rain."

"Just do as I say."

The sinner went into the churchyard and came back ten minutes later soaked to the skin. "I kept looking up at heaven but I didn't get a revelation. I'm just wet and I feel like an idiot."

"Not bad," the minister said. "That's quite a revelation for a first try."

8
NOT-SO-SILENT PRAYER

James 5:16 says, "The effectual fervent prayer of a righteous man availeth much." *Among those blessings that prayer availeth is laughter.*

Shortly after the U.S. Supreme Court outlawed prayer in public schools, a pupil in class heard her teacher sneeze.

"God bless you," the girl said.

"Cut that out," the teacher replied, "or we'll both be in trouble."

Ken Murray said of the Supreme Court decision. "It's a shame. Now that there's no more praying in the schools, kids will have to go to motels to read the Bible."

He added, "If this keeps up, the Gideons will have to go underground."

There's still a sign in a California public school that reads: IN CASE OF ATOMIC ATTACK, THE FEDERAL RULING CONCERNING PRAYER IN THIS BUILDING WILL BE TEMPORARILY SUSPENDED.

A *Look* magazine cartoon showed a pro-prayer congressman reading a bill to his colleagues and saying, "My amendment will authorize any child to use the school telephone to Dial-A-Prayer."

Pulitzer prize-winning cartoonist Paul Conrad drew a panel in the Los Angeles *Times* which showed pupils staring at a blackboard on which was chalked: NONDENOMINATIONAL PRAYER.

The caption for the children's prayer read:

"To whom it may concern: Our something-or-other, who art in somewhere-or-other, hallowed be thy what-cha-ma-call-it. . . ."

When he appeared as a commencement speaker at Miami University in Oxford, Ohio, in 1970, Bob Hope said from the rostrum: "It was a little easier to get through school in my day. The questions were just as hard, but praying was still legal."

In Grand Prairie, Texas, located between Dallas and Fort Worth, a heavy storm came up, relates Dr. Warren Walker.

"Pray, pray," the wife beseeched her husband.

The husband, who was not a man of faith, did the best he could.

"Lord," he said, "this is Will Thompson, of Grand Prairie, Texas. If this storm doesn't let up we're going to see You in just a little bit."

Evangelist Arthur Blessitt was the guest of this writer's family at dinner one evening.

Eight-year-old Diane Wagner was asked to say grace. Recalling her visit to the Sunset Strip where she'd seen the Reverend Blessitt ministering to hippies, she prayed, "Jesus, bless this food, and do Thy thing!"

The minister on the golf course missed a very easy putt. He looked to heaven and uttered a brief prayer, "Lord, You don't have to help me, but You sure don't have to hurt me."

A church in New York City that sponsors a Dial-a-Prayer service became entangled in telephone company inefficiency, which caused a sharp drop in the number of calls.

The minister commented, "Our problem is that we know many have called, but few were connected."

The young minister, filled with pride at the forthcoming publication of his first book, went into the pulpit and began his prayer: "O Thou who hast also written a Book . . . ."

A minister's slip of the tongue resulted in this prayer:

"May everyone in our church come to Jesus and be filled with veal and zigor."

The minister suddenly realized he had forgotten to invite a particularly touchy woman parishioner to his church-sponsored picnic.

When he called her at the last minute, she said: "It's too late. I've already prayed for rain!"

"Do you say grace before eating?" the Sunday-school teacher asked the little boy.

"It ain't necessary," he answered. "My mom is a good cook."

The minister and his wife were entertaining a dozen guests. At ten P.M., the minister told his daughter to go to bed. He reminded her not to forget her prayers.

"Okay," she said as she addressed all the guests, "anybody need anything?"

The eight-year-old boy had misbehaved and his father spanked him.

"Now, before you go to bed say your prayers," the father ordered.

"I'm sorry, God," the boy prayed, "that I was bad. Bless Mommy, bless my brother, sister, and my teacher. And don't forget to bless Grandma and Grandpa."

Still smarting from the whipping, the boy turned to his father and said, "I suppose you noticed you wasn't in my prayer."

In church for the first time the small girl was wide-eyed with astonishment as the congregation kneeled and bowed their heads.

"Mom, what are they doing?"

"They're getting ready to say their prayers."

"With all their clothes on?"

The young boy in Houston, Texas, missed his father who'd been on a long business trip to California.

He began his nightly prayer by saying, "Our Father, who art in Los Angeles . . . ."

The children in the Sunday-school class had recited The Lord's Prayer dozens of times and they had all memorized it. Now the teacher wanted to see if each could write it out.

The paper from one youngster contained the phrases: "Harold be Thy Name"; "Give us this day our jelly bread"; and "Lead us not into Penn Station."

The minister saw a youngster pulling his toy wagon along the street with a statue of Jesus in it.

"Why are you doing that?"

"The week before Christmas I prayed to Jesus for a wagon. And I told Him if He'd bring me one, I'd give Him a ride around the block."

"Do you say your prayers every night?" the minister asked the little girl.

"No, not every night. Some nights I don't want anything."

The nine-year-old girl prayed: "Dear God, take care of my family, take care of the whole world. And please God, take care of Yourself, or we're all sunk."

"Dear God, I want to pray to you tonight in the unforgettable words of Jesus in the Book of John." There was a pause while the minister hesitated. ". . . But I forgot them."

The preacher was given to supplications that were nearly as long and boring as his sermons, causing one member of his congregation to sigh: "I wonder whatever happened to silent prayer."

Another preacher in his daily prayer had a more practical approach:

> Lord fill my mouth with worthwhile stuff,
> And nudge me when I've said enough.

Pastor Harold Hamlet, of the First Baptist Church of Lakeside, California, passes on the story about the preacher who had "quitting" meetings every New Year's Eve. All the members of the church would gather for prayer and song and the preacher would ask them to get up and tell the congregation what they were going to quit doing in the new year.

At one meeting a man said he was going to quit drinking and pray more. Another man said he was going to quit swearing and pray more. A third member said he was going to quit smoking and pray more. Everyone in the congregation said they were going to quit something and pray more except one middle-aged woman.

"I pray every day," she said, "and I ain't been doing nothing wrong, so I guess I'll have to quit doing that."

Reverend Bill H. Lewis, pastor of the Temple Baptist Church, of Santa Barbara, California, says he heard about a teenager who was asked to give a prayer at the beginning of the service.

"And dear God," he said, "please save a lot of people tonight from our pastor's preaching."

When he was appointed a bishop in the Anglican Church, the clergy-man prayed, "Lord, I feel rather like a mosquito in a nudist camp. I know what I ought to do, but I don't know where to begin."

The evening lesson at the prayer meeting was from the Book of Job. As the minister read, "Yea, the light of the wicked shall be put out . . ." a fuse blew, and the church was left in total darkness.

"Brothers and sisters," the pastor said, recovering quickly, "in view of the sudden and startling fulfillment of this prophecy, we will spend a few minutes in silent prayer for the electric light company."

One of her three small sons had misbehaved. As she put them to bed, the mother said: "I'm going to say my prayers and ask God which one of you was bad. Wouldn't the guilty one like to tell me before I ask God?"

One of the boys answered, "No, Mom, let's wait and see what God has to say."

The slight mispronunciation in the tot's prayer was nonetheless applicable: "Give us this day our daily breath."

The prayer of one consumer-activist housewife: "Give us this day our daily bread, free of cadmium, mercury, and lead."

The prayer of an inflation-ridden family, "Father, we thank Thee for this bounty You have placed before us, despite the steadily rising price index."

The frugal housewife was serving leftovers for the third consecutive night.

"Don't forget to bless the food," she told her husband.

"Darling," he answered, "I'll be happy to if you can show me one morsel that hasn't already been blessed twice."

"Dear Brother," said the relieved missionary, "how delightful it is to join you in prayer when a moment ago I feared for my life."

"Don't interrupt," said the lion. "I'm saying grace."

The four-year-old girl was holding her kitten in her lap. "Listen, Mommy, he's saying his purrs."

The skinflint vice-president told his office manager, "I hear you've been going over my head."

"No, sir. I haven't talked to the president of the company."

"That isn't what I mean. Someone told me you've been praying for a raise."

The Sunday-school class was asked to give a definition of prayer.

"Prayer," said a small girl, "is messages telephoned to heaven at nights and on Sundays, when the rates are lower."

"Dear God," the little boy prayed, "now that I can read, will You write me a letter?"

A forecaster for the National Weather Service offered this explanation for an unexpected snowstorm in the ski country outside Los Angeles:

"My kids were going to Lake Arrowhead for a weekend church retreat. They kept telling me they were hoping they'd have snow. They got it all right, eleven inches.

"I guess it was just a case of too many people praying too hard—and they overdid it."

Feminist leader Gloria Steinem was once asked if she believed in God.

"Certainly," she replied, "I pray to Her quite frequently."

As they entered the *on*-ramp of the Hollywood Freeway during rush hour traffic, the minister told his wife: "Keep driving, dear, and I'll keep praying."

When someone asked a California wine-maker if his brother, who was a minister, objected to his profession, he replied, "We have a perfect relationship. He prays for my soul, and I drink to his health."

"And, please," said the boy in his invocation to God, "send some clothes to those poor ladies in my daddy's magazines."

Another boy said in his nightly prayer: "Dear God. We had a good time at church today. I wish You could have been there."

Mrs. Billy Graham in a speech to a group of women in Minneapolis confided, "God has not always answered my prayers. If He had, I would have married the wrong man—several times."

The Christmas shopping tour the little girl had taken with her parents had been hectic. It took an hour to find a parking place in the shopping center, the stores were crowded with shouting, shoving people, and the clerks had all been rude.

That evening the girl prayed, "Dear God, forgive us our Christmases as we forgive those who Christmas against us."

Worried about a tough exam the next day, the teenager prayed, "Lord, don't let anything come my way that You and I can't handle together."

There's humor—and more—in this prayer written by an anonymous senior citizen.

Please, dear Lord, give us the strength to rise above hurt feelings when, for weeks, we do not receive so much as a telephone call from our children. We must remember they are busy with *their* children, with bridge, golf, shopping, bowling, business acquaintances, and social friends.

When our grandchildren are present, help us remain silent so we do not miss a single word of their wisdom, for through some mysterious process they have managed to learn everything there is to know. Strike us dumb in the presence of these young people, Heavenly Father, that we may not utter a word against their hair, dress, music or frequent use of four-letter words.

Help us, dear Lord, to hold our tongues about our experiences of the past, lest we become tiresome and boring. Keep us, Heavenly Father, in good health and high spirits, so that when our children or grandchildren need attention and encouragement we are available.

Dear Lord, keep us solvent so that we may forever be able to maintain our independence and not be a burden.

And, above all, dear Lord, help us, as we come closer to You with each passing day, to keep our sense of humor.

The busy Indianapolis minister was visiting a woman parishioner in a hospital. In his pocket, he carried an electronic device that notified him when he was needed. He began his prayer, "Dear Lord . . ." and was interrupted by three beeps from the device.

The smiling woman said, "My goodness. I've never known a pastor who had such direct contact."

The expectant mother asked her young son to pray for her when she went to the hospital.

She gave birth to triplets, and when she returned home her son said, "Gosh, Mom aren't you glad I stopped praying when I did?"

The prayer of a six-year-old girl whose father was home after hospital surgery: "Please God, don't let it hurt my daddy if anyone jumps on his bed . . . because it will probably be me."

The multimillionaire invited his five married daughters to dinner. When they were all seated at the table, he said, "I'm a very old man. God has given me a great deal, but I've always been disappointed that I have no grandchildren. I'm drawing up my will tomorrow and leaving a $100,000 bonus to the first of my daughters who presents me with a grandchild. Now I'm going to say grace."

He bowed his head and said a short prayer. When he looked up, everyone was gone.

The youngster, who'd just received a new radio for his birthday, was asked to say grace.

"We thank Thee, God," he prayed, "for all Thy blessings. *Amen* and *FM*."

Two friends, both inveterate racetrack bettors, decided to attend church to pray for winners.

When they emerged from the church one said to the other, "The word is *hallulujah* not *Hialeah!*"

The man at the racetrack was beseeching God for a winner. When his horse rounded the last turn and was fifteen lengths ahead, he said, "Thanks, Lord . . . I'll take it from here."

Abraham Lincoln often prayed for divine guidance. As he put it once, "I have been driven to my knees many times by the overwhelming conviction that I had nowhere else to go."

Said Herbert Hoover: "Presidents have only two moments of personal seclusion. One is prayer. The other is fishing—and they cannot pray all the time!"

A self-made man recalls, "When times were hard in my family—as they often were—our prayers went up to God, but never to Washington."

Television personality Bill Moyers, formerly a Baptist minister, was one of President Lyndon Johnson's key aides.

At a luncheon one day with the president in attendance, Moyers prayed in a quiet voice.

"Speak up, Bill, I can't hear a word."

"Mr. President," Moyers said, "I wasn't talking to you."

Wisconsin legislator Stanley York, who is a minister, delivered this invocation to the state assembly: "O Lord, you have given us minds and you have given us mouths. Help us keep the two connected."

When Reverend Robert Bock of North Hollywood, California, was chosen to give the opening prayer at the convening of the U.S. Senate in 1973, he received these instructions from the senate chaplain:

"Make it less than 150 words. Don't touch on anything controversial. And remember that senators, because of the wisdom of God, already are the most prayed-over group in the world."

Dr. Edward Gardiner Latch, a genial Methodist minister, while he was the official chaplain to the House of Representatives often counseled congressmen.

He learned the wisdom of not giving advice to politicians.

"I just listen and help if I can," he said. "Most of all I don't preach to them, I pray for them."

9

THE LORD LOVETH A CHEERFUL GIVER

Clergymen and parishioners have learned to their sorrow and joy the truth of English novelist Henry Fielding's remark: "Make money your God, and it will plague you like the devil."

Bob Harrington tells about the family that returned from church and everybody was complaining about the service. Father didn't think the preaching was any good. Mother didn't like the choir. The teenage daughter said the benches were hard.

The little boy in the family spoke up finally and said, "I don't know what all of you expected for a dollar."

A minister was annoyed that a member of his congregation had spent more money decorating the exterior of his house for Christmas than he'd contributed to the church all year.

"What I really resent," the minister told one of his deacons, "is his holly-er-than-thou attitude."

The doctor sent a note to his minister: "Sorry I haven't tithed for three months. But, you know, there's a lot of that going around."

A minister once observed: "More tithes are inspired by cowardice than generosity."

The church was hard pressed for funds and the pastor called a parishioner who'd failed to tithe in some time.

"I'm surprised I haven't heard from you concerning your financial obligation to the church," the pastor said.

"There's no reason to be surprised, Pastor. I haven't sent anything."

The minister was called in for the reading of the will of the wealthy businessman in his congregation who had died.

The minister and the man's relatives were all disappointed to hear the succinct contents of the will: "Being of sound mind and body, I spent it all."

The preacher and his wife were having a spat about the family budget.

The next day the preacher's wife, the mother of six children, phoned her mother and said, "He doesn't see why *I* can't feed the multitude with two fishes and a few loaves of bread."

The minister didn't blush about the invitation he received to preach in a nudist camp.

"After all," he told a friend, "they're God's people, too. But I wonder where they keep the collection money."

"Friends," said the minister, "I have in my hands a hundred-dollar sermon that lasts ten minutes, a fifty-dollar sermon that lasts twenty minutes, and a twenty-dollar sermon that lasts a full hour. We will now take up the collection and see which one I will deliver."

A prominent parishioner was aghast at the dreadful financial condition of the church.

He told the minister, "We've tried grab bags, box socials, benefits —everything. What else is there to try?"

"Maybe," said the minister, "we ought to try religion."

The small boy was reporting to a friend on the size of the offerings in his father's church.

"Gosh, he must be rich," the friend said.

"You bet. Some Sundays he even has two or three five-and-ten dollar bills."

Will Rogers said: "Noah must have taken into the Ark two taxes, one male and one female. And did they multiply beautifully! Next to the guinea pigs, taxes have been the most prolific animals."

The minister placed a sign on the church bulletin board: REMEMBER, IT IS MORE BLESSED TO GIVE THAN TO RECEIVE. BESIDES, YOU DON'T HAVE TO WRITE THANK-YOU NOTES.

On Saturday night, while shopping downtown, the pastor accidently spotted a member of his congregation with a woman who wasn't his wife.

After his sermon the next day, the minister declared, "Brethren, in the offering this morning I'll expect more giving than we've had in the past. I know for a fact there's one sinner in the congregation that was out last night with a woman he wasn't married to. Now, if he can spend money on sin, he can contribute at least ten dollars to the church."

When the minister counted the collection later, he was astonished to find *fifteen* ten-dollar bills.

There was also a five-dollar bill that had a note pinned to it: "Pastor, this is all I got left, but I'll give you the rest next Sunday. Please don't tell my wife."

The rich but uneducated farmer told the president of the Bible college that he was planning a sizable donation to a rival school.

"That's all right, but I think you should know that before a student can go to that school he has to matriculate in the teacher's office."

"I'll be doggoned," the farmer said.

"And you should also know that the boys and girls use the same curriculum!"

"I can't believe it."

"What's more, before a student can get a degree from that school, he has to have his thesis examined by the faculty!"

The farmer said, "They'll never get a dime from me!"

One Sunday the usher dropped the collection plate and the coins and bills scattered all over the aisle.

The congregation tittered, so the usher thought he should explain.

"I couldn't help dropping the plate—I was just too excited. I've never seen a hundred-dollar bill before."

The collection was unusually small, and the minister wondered why.

A deacon explained: "I think you got yourself a little mixed up when you asked for the love offering."

"What did I say?"

"That it's more blessed to receive than to give."

At the close of a church convention, a hotel bellhop complained about one minister: "He came here with ten ten-dollar bills and the Ten Commandments. And he didn't break any of them."

"And speaking of an up-to-date church," the minister announced, "I've got good news for those of you with credit cards . . . ."

The debt-ridden minister's wife told him, "Dear, in next week's sermon I wish you'd stop moralizing on what money can't buy—and list a few things that it can."

A Los Angeles *Times* cartoon showed a stork in flight. The caption said: "I'm carrying a boy. What with the cost of sugar and spice and everything nice, I don't deliver many little girls anymore."

"There's one nice thing about working for the Lord," says a minister. "The pay isn't much, but the retirement plan is fantastic!"

The minister advised a member of his congregation who was a policeman newly assigned to crowd-control duty: "The quickest way to scatter a mob is to take off your hat and start taking up a collection."

"Pastor, I want you to know your sermon was wonderful. I can find nothing but praise for you and your church."

"So I noticed when the offering plate was passed."

The stockbroker was recommending a modest investment portfolio to the minister.

"Are you sure these are all blue chips?" the minister asked.

"They're better than blue chips," the broker replied, "this is my Holier-Than-Dow list."

"Money isn't everything," the minister sighed as he looked at the red ink in the church budget. "And I wish I had a dollar for every time I've said that."

The church member was delinquent in paying his pledge so the minister told him, "You're a good man. I know you pay your debts to everyone else. Why not pay your debts to the Lord?"

"To tell you the truth, Preacher," the man answered, "He just don't push as hard as some of the others."

The parishioner said, "Reverend, if I contributed $1 million to your church, what's the first thing you would buy?"

"Kathryn Kuhlman's book, *I Believe in Miracles*."

A lawyer's son and a minister's son were talking.

The lawyer's son said, "My father talks to people for an hour and they pay him one hundred dollars."

Said the minister's son, "That's nothing. My father talks for only half an hour and it takes twelve men to carry all the money to him."

The eight-year-old boy asked his mother for an advance on his allowance.

"What for?"

"Our Sunday-school teacher is leaving and the kids want to give her a little momentum."

A rabbi, a priest, and a minister were discussing church funds.

The rabbi said, "After our collection, I draw a big circle and throw all the collection money into the air. Whatever lands inside the circle we use for God's work. Whatever lands outside the circle we use for ourselves."

The priest said he followed precisely the same procedure in his church.

"In our church," the minister said, "we believe in miracles. We also draw a circle and throw the money into the air. Then we let God decide how much He wants to keep."

"Were you a good little girl at church this morning?" the mother inquired of her daughter.

"Yes, ma'm. A nice man offered me a big plate full of money, but I said, 'No, thank you, sir.' "

A church worker who was soliciting money for foreign missions approached the town skinflint.

"I never give a dime for missionary work," the miserly man said.

The worker held out the bag he was using for contributions and said, "In that case, help yourself to some of this. It's for heathens like you."

"I need one hundred dollars to get out of debt," the man told his minister. "I keep praying to God for help but He doesn't send it."

"Don't lose faith," the minister urged. "Keep praying."

The minister thought about his parishioner's plight, and though he didn't earn much money himself, he decided to help by giving the man fifty dollars from his own pocket.

He met the man a few days later and said, "Here, God sent this to you."

When he got home, the man prayed, "Thank You, Lord. But next time you send money, don't send it through the minister. He kept half of it."

The minister wrote to one of the world's richest men, asking for a donation to his church.

The billionaire sent a check for ten dollars.

"I don't know whether to cash it or frame it," said the disappointed clergyman.

In Las Vegas, a well-known, big-time gambler died. At the church service, a friend gave the eulogy. "George isn't dead," he said. "He's only sleeping."

"I've got a hundred dollars that says he doesn't wake up," a voice from a rear pew declared.

The estranged husband of a woman who won $130,000 in the Irish Sweepstakes went to court and asked for a portion of her winnings.

The judge ruled against him, saying "What God giveth, man taketh not away."

While she was prime minister of Israel, Golda Meir proposed a social-welfare budget of $294 million before the parliament.

"The miracle of Israel has to be for the whole people as one," Mrs. Meir said.

One parliamentarian added quietly, "The only trouble is that it will take a miracle to accomplish that miracle."

When Mrs. Meir was in Los Angeles several years ago to raise money for Israel, her reception at the Beverly Hills Hotel was warm and emotional. The ballroom where the fund-raising dinner was held was packed with many of the city's wealthiest people.

As the appeal for pledges began, there were promises of $1,000, $5,000, $10,000, $25,000. One man promised $100,000.

When the spotlight fell on Harry Gelbart, who is a barber with many movie-star customers, he found himself with only a $100 bill, which he promptly sent up to the dais.

After the pledge-taking ended, more than $1 million had been promised. Harry left quietly. The next morning producer Dore Schary called him and asked, "Why did you leave so quickly? Golda Meir wanted to meet the barber who gave $100."

Harry wasn't at a loss for an explanation of Mrs. Meir's interest in him. "It proves cash is one thing, promises another."

The wife of the minister told him as he sat down to dinner, "We can't afford the high-priced spread anymore. So, instead we're using butter."

Edith and Archie Bunker were discussing a friend who'd become rich in the used-car business.

Archie said that even though the man was a millionaire, he didn't like him.

"Why not?" Edith asked. "He's a very nice man, and so thoughtful. He never forgets to send us a Christmas card. Last year it was the Prince of Peace driving a blue convertible."

The penny-pinching woman parishioner had died. Several days later, her daughter came to see the minister in his office.

"I have a message for you from heaven from my mother," the daughter said.

The minister asked: "Did she call collect?"

A Chicago clergyman reported to police that two youths had robbed his church of $120 and hit him over the head with a brandy bottle.

The police said the brand name on the bottle was Christian Brothers.

Billy Graham received the following letter:

How I admire you. I want to be of help in your worldwide movement, so I'm enclosing my check for the full amount that I can afford to give.

I made the check out for forty-five dollars. The reason I'm not signing it is that I want to remain anonymous.

The minister looked balefully at the collection plate, and told a member of his board, "Most people in our congregation think the church is like a laundromat—coin-operated."

A letter to "Dear Abby" from a reader, defending the cost of maintaining a church, said in part:

Churches can't live on air. Religion, like water, may be free, but when they pipe it to you, you've got to help pay for the piping. And the piper.

The minister's wife was telling a friend about her household budget. "I spend 40 percent of our income for food, 30 percent for shelter, 30 percent for clothing and 20 percent for transportation and incidentals."

"But that makes 120 per cent."

Resignation in her voice, she said, "Don't I know it!"

The amount of money that members of a congregation leave to the church in their wills, says one minister, is a dead giveaway.

He didn't get the "blessings, benefits, and rewards" the pastor's sermons had promised, so the parishioner sued his church for the return of eight hundred dollars in tithes.

Asked what manna he had expected from heaven, the man said, "I'm not sure, but God better think of something."

California legislators were about to debate a bill that would mean a whopping new tax increase. This was the invocation of Reverend Robert Romeis, chaplain of the state senate: "Almighty God, we have been told that two things are certain—death and taxes. It doesn't seem that the Senate of California can do much about the former, but we beseech You that they do nothing about the latter."

The measure failed to pass.

The backslider asked his minister: "Does the government allow you to deduct the wages of sin as a business expense?"

An Internal Revenue agent telephoned a minister and said, "I'm going over the return of one of your members." The agent told the minister the man's name. "He lists a donation of two thousand dollars to the church. Can you tell if he made that contribution?"

The minister said: "I don't have my records in front of me—but if he didn't, he will!"

Asked the meaning of the word *budget,* a boy in Sunday school answered, "It's a family quarrel."

The minister listened patiently as the woman parishioner told him that her husband was angry because she'd run up extravagant bills with her dozen credit cards. "What should I do?" she wondered.

"Discontinue the cards. If the Good Lord had meant for you to carry all those cards, He'd have given you a pouch."

This story appeared in pastor Jack Taylor's *Church Bell* newsletter:
A son at college wrote his father,
　　Dear Dad, You haven't sent me a check in two weeks. What sort of Christian kindness is that?
His father replied,
　　Dear Son, That is known as unremitting Christian kindness.

Then there was the minister who tacked a sign on the church bulletin board, which read: THE LORD LOVETH A CHEERFUL GIVER. HE ALSO ACCEPTS FROM A GROUCH.

10
ADAM'S RIB RIBBED

The Book of Proverbs says a virtuous woman is a price far above rubies. So is the Christian mirth that women have inspired and uttered.

The minister announced from the pulpit that a member of the congregation "has had a loud-speaker system installed in our church in loving memory of his wife."

Pastor Richard D. Cunningham tells about the time he laboriously instructed everyone in the wedding party that it was vital not to make any mistakes because the bride would cherish the memory of the occasion all her life.

"The rehearsals," he says, "went off without a hitch. And the ceremony was carried out to perfection by everyone with the exception of yours truly. I addressed the bride as *Debbie*. Her name was *Cathy*."

This announcement appeared in an Abilene Christian College newsletter:

"After waiting seven years for Maxwell House to perk, we decided to try instant."

Mr. and Mrs. Joe Maxwell explained they'd adopted twin girls.

Says one wise minister, "Being a good husband is similar to being a preacher. It helps if you like your Boss."

Another minister who was counseling a distraught wife asked: "Did you wake up grumpy this morning?"

"No," she said, "I let him sleep."

The preacher and a member of his congregation were discussing marriage.

"You say you've been married twenty-five years and your wife still looks like a newlywed?" the minister asked.

"No, I said we'd been married twenty-five years and she still *cooks* like a newlywed."

In Louisville, Kentucky, not long ago a man who was one-hundred-years old took a bride of eighty-six.

As he walked up the aisle, he was heard to comment wryly, "The preacher better not stretch it out too long."

There are times when the path of true love does indeed run smooth.

A minister reports he attended a golden wedding celebration and the subject of reincarnation was mentioned. One of the children of the long-married couple asked her father, "If you could be reincarnated, who would you like to be?"

He replied without hesitation: "Your mother's next husband."

The bride shocked the church organist with the song she insisted she wanted played at her wedding: "What Kind of Fool Am I?"

The minister asked the bride, "Do you take this man for richer, for poorer, for better, for worse?"

At which point a twice-divorced woman whispered to her friend, "You know, I've never been too crazy about those odds."

A pastor once observed, "If a man says marriage hasn't changed him, he's probably not out of the church yet."

Reverend Bill Gothard of Oak Brook, Illinois was once asked how, as a bachelor, he could advise husbands and wives on marriage and child rearing problems.

The Reverend Gothard answered: "We have some pretty good precedents for that: Jesus Christ and the Apostle Paul."

There obviously was something lacking in the account of one wedding as reported by the Greenfield, Massachusetts, *Recorder-Gazette:* "In the church ceremony, the bride wore an aquamarine floor-length gown with fuchsia trimming and carried an old fashioned."

The couple who'd been married for twenty years were having a heated argument.

The husband said, "Don't you remember promising to love, honor, and obey?"

"Of course I do," she replied, "What else could I do? I didn't want to make a scene in church."

Says columnist Earl Wilson, "Too bad some marriage ceremonies now omit the word *obey*. It was the only thing that lent a little humor to the occasion."

A bereaved husband ordered a tombstone with the inscription: THE LIGHT OF MY LIFE HAS GONE OUT.

Soon after, he remarried, and not wishing to offend his second wife, he had the inscription changed to read: THE LIGHT OF MY LIFE HAS GONE OUT—BUT I HAVE STRUCK A NEW MATCH.

The wife was complaining to her minister: "Just this morning my husband said I was a terrible housekeeper. I got so angry I ran into the . . . uh . . . what do you call it?—oh, yes, the kitchen."

A minister who has married hundreds of couples and advised many of them says: "I've learned that only two things are necessary to keep a wife happy. First, let her think she's having her way. Second, let her have it."

"The best way to save a marriage," said cynic W. C. Fields, "is not to show up in church for the wedding."

The woman told her pastor, "It's a shame that we have such a high rate of divorce in the country. I wouldn't think of divorcing my husband. Why, he's just like one of the family."

During his sermon on marriage, the minister pointed out: "A guilty conscience is what makes you tell your wife something you know she'll find out anyway."

Since the onset of the Women's Liberation Movement, feminists have sought to change many of the biblical mandates concerning the relationship of men and women, as well as the gender of God.

Billy Graham was picketed at the Rose Parade in Pasadena, California, by a group of militant feminists. Mr. Graham was criticized for his view "that the Bible relegated women to the role of housewife and mother."

One protestor's sign read:

IF GOD WANTED WOMEN IN THE KITCHEN, SHE WOULD HAVE GIVEN THEM ALUMINUM HANDS.

The Reverend Robert Drinan, who is a congressman from Massachusetts, bought a T-shirt at a benefit for Women's Lib reading: TRUST IN GOD. SHE WILL PROVIDE.

According to one wit, a woman has truly reached Women's Lib status when *she's* the one who forgets the wedding anniversary.

The Reverend John Brynell, a British minister, tells of reluctantly helping his wife with the dishes.

"This isn't a man's job," he protested

"Yes, it is," his wife said, quoting 2 Kings 21:13; " 'And I will wipe Jerusalem as a man wipeth a dish, wiping it, and turning it upside down.' "

The pro-Women's Lib Reverend A. W. Behrens, of St. John's Church in Bancroft, Iowa, was asked to offer a prayer to the state legislature.

His prayer included the plea: "Please Lord, let's keep the male chauvinism up and down the aisle to a minimum."

"This is a tough problem," said the female executive, who was a committed Women's Libber. "To solve it will take the wisdom of a Sheba."

A feminist and a man who didn't believe in Women's Lib were debating the subject.

The feminist asked: "After all, what's the difference between you and a woman?"

"I cannot conceive," he answered smoothly.

Not all women, of course, are feminists.

One woman asks: "What would have become of the human race had Eve rejected motherhood in favor of pursuing a more gratifying career in the already-promising apple industry?"

Some modern weddings are being held in unusual locations.

A Utah minister was flown by helicopter to the top of 12,000-foot Mount Timpanogos. After the ceremony, the bridegroom gave his bride the traditional kiss and said, "I always promised that if you married me, I'd take you to the heights."

A minister who performed a wedding in the hills overlooking Malibu, California, reported, "The bride got herself a husband and poison ivy."

More than one minister has heard the woeful complaint from a wife whose husband has retired: "I married him for better or worse—but not for lunch."

The divinity student was telling his seatmate on the plane, "I got married because I was tired of going to the laundromat, eating in restaurants, and wearing socks with holes."

"That's funny," the man said, "I got divorced for the same reasons."

One man admits his wife tends to dominate him. He told a friend, "When we went to the minister of our church for counseling, she told her side of the story—and then she told my side of the story."

The life of Dr. Norman Vincent Peale was made into a movie called *One Man's Way*.

When he and his wife attended the premiere, they were both particularly interested in the love scenes between the actor and the actress who were portraying them.

Mrs. Peale said, "I don't recall our romance being nearly so exciting."

"You must remember, dear," said Dr. Peale, "they are professionals and we were only amateurs."

Edith Bunker, returning home after church, told Archie: "The minister gave a sermon about marriage. He said it's made in heaven. Do you think our marriage was made in heaven?"

"No—in Japan!" said Archie with his usual distemper.

After the wedding, the minister told the groom, "Son, God bless you. You're at the end of your troubles."

A year passed and the young man was back with the news that he was thinking of getting a divorce. "Remember, you told me when you married us that I was at the end of all my troubles."

Smiling, the minister said, "Son, I just didn't tell you which end."

Billy Graham tells the story of the North Carolina minister who was preaching a sermon about perfection.

The minister said, "Jesus was not only the Son of God, but He was the only perfect Man in this history of the world. Anybody ever hear of another perfect man?"

A fellow stood up and said, "According to my wife, her ex-husband was."

A hard-bitten oil driller received an urgent call from his minister who told him his wife had been rushed to the hospital.

The minister added, "The doctor's going to need your permission for an exploratory operation."

"Nothing doing," the oilman said. "Nobody's goin' to wildcat on my wife."

A Sunday-school teacher got on a bus in Los Angeles. The man next to her had obviously imbibed a few too many.

As she was preparing a geography lesson about the Holy Land for her class, she opened her purse, took out a map, unfolded it and started to study it intently.

The drunk stared at the map and tapped her on the shoulder. "Lady," he said, "you're on the wrong bus!"

An understanding minister once said, "For untold ages women have been famous for untold ages."

Dr. Warren Walker recalls the minister who noted during his sermon, "It is a statistical fact that married men live longer than single men."

One man spoke up and said: "Preacher, it just seems longer."

One comedy writer says, "I've got nothing against women. I just happen to believe that when Eve was created in the Garden of Eden, the snake nudged Adam and said, "Well, there goes the neighborhood."

From the Baptist *Reflector:*

Adam to Eve as they fled from the Garden of Eden, "Honey, don't worry about this—we're living in a changing society."

It's been said that Eve was the first person who ate herself out of house and home.

It's also been said that beauty contests did not start in Atlantic City. They began when the second woman arrived on earth.

An elderly woman was asked at a church celebration in Los Angeles in 1974 why she'd lived to the age of 105.

"Well," she said, "mainly because I was born in 1869."

Bob Harrington says that the unisex trend in dress and hair has mystified him. After he married a hippie couple in New Orleans, he threw up his hands in despair and said, "Now, one of you kiss the bride."

"How come Aunt Martha never married?" the boy asked his mother.

"Well, son, she was two-thirds married once. She was in the church, the minister was in the church, but the man never showed up."

On their way to a church Bible class, the husband asked, "Are you planning to ask any questions?"

"Certainly! Why do you think I had my hair done?"

"Don't you have an appointment with the minister," the husband asked his wife.

"Yes, I do, but I told him I'd be late so I've lots of time yet."

The wares of the Fuller Brush man were enticing to the housewife at the door.

"I can't really afford to buy anything," she said, "so don't lead me into temptation."

"Madam," the salesman replied politely, "I am not leading you into temptation but delivering you from evil."

The woman agreed and bought three brushes.

Said a woman at a prayer meeting, "I ain't what I ought to be, and I ain't what I'm goin' to be—but anyway, I ain't what I was!"

According to Chaplain Ray, "When the Lord handed out humor, woman was late, as usual. But she arrived just in time to get the last laugh."

11
LAST WRITES

THIS STONE WAS RAISED BY SARAH'S LORD,
NOT SARAH'S VIRTUES TO RECORD
FOR THEY'RE WELL KNOWN TO ALL THE TOWN;
IT WAS RAISED TO KEEP HER DOWN.

Such lively tombstone inscriptions, unfortunately, are a lost art. The golden age of the imaginative epitaph disappeared following World War II. Prior to that, Americans, before passing to their reward, often took their humor, cynicism, joy, prejudices, hatred, or love to the graveyard with them.

On the tombstone of a sailor buried in Connecticut:

POOR JACK'S MAIN TOPSAIL
IS LAID TO THE MAST,
THE WORMS GNAW HIS TIMBERS,
HIS VESSEL A WRECK,
BUT WHEN THE LAST WHISTLE SOUNDS
HE'LL BE UP ON DECK.

A ship's captain from Rhode Island perhaps should never have switched professions. He left his ironic last testament in a Methodist cemetery:

ERECTED
IN MEMORY OF
CAPT. THOMAS STETSON
WHO WAS KILLED BY THE FALL
OF A TREE NOVEMBER 28, 1820.

NEARLY 30 YEARS HE WAS MASTER
OF A VESSEL AND LEFT THAT
EMPLOYMENT AT THE AGE
OF 48 FOR THE LESS HAZARDOUS
ONE OF CULTIVATING HIS FARM.

The widow of a man named William Strange, who was born in West Virginia, erected a monument to her husband after he was lost at sea.

STRANGE IS MY NAME AND I'M ON STRANGE GROUND.
AND STRANGE IT IS I CAN'T BE FOUND.

A New Hampshire farmer who'd evidently jousted with good and evil had this couplet inscribed on his stone:

THE LAND I CLEARED IS NOW MY GRAVE
THINK WELL MY FRIENDS HOW YOU BEHAVE.

With typical Vermont brevity, a seventy-four-year-old man had a single word inscribed on his marble slab:

TRANSPLANTED.

There was little doubt that one Connecticut gentleman who wrote his own epitaph had a sense of humor to the end.

UNDER THIS SOD,
UNDER THESE TREES
LIES THE BODY OF JONATHAN PEASE.
HE IS NOT HERE
BUT ONLY HIS POD.
HE HAS SHELLED OUT HIS PEAS
AND GONE TO HIS GOD.

A world-weary New Englander wrote:

> GONE TO A BETTER LAND
> I HOPE.

Slightly more cavalier is this tombstone:

> IF THERE IS ANOTHER WORLD
> I LIVE IN BLISS.
> IF NOT ANOTHER
> I HAVE MADE THE MOST OF THIS.

The following message, on the grave of John Taylor, can still be seen by visitors to a cemetery in Massachusetts:

> DEATH HAS DECOMPOSED HIM
> AND AT THE GREAT RESURRECTION CHRIST
> WILL RECOMPOSE HIM.

Hundreds of tombstones, particularly in New England, bear this familiar warning to make peace with God:

> BEHOLD MY FRIENDS AS YOU PASS BY
> AS YOU ARE NOW SO ONCE WAS I
> AS I AM NOW, SO YOU MUST BE
> PREPARE FOR DEATH AND FOLLOW ME.

An Ohio man knew his exact destination:

> HE WHO WROTE THIS DID IT WELL
> THE DEVIL IS WAITING FOR ME IN HELL.

On the grave of a sickly New York woman who thought she might regain her health in Florida:

> SHE LEFT HER HOME IN SEARCH
> OF HEALTH
> BUT DIED ANYWAY.

The epitaph of a seventeen-year-old Boston youngster:

> KILLED BY THE KICK
>   OF A HORSE
> GONE TO A BETTER WORLD
>   OF COURSE.

In another Boston cemetery:

> NEARBY THESE GRAY ROCKS
> ENCLOSED IN A BOX
> LIES MARY COX
> WHO DIED OF SMALLPOX
> AND NONE TOO SOON FOR HER
> HUSBAND, WILLIAM COX.

In Macon, Georgia, the marker of a long-gone seventy-eight-year-old relates:

> BEEN HERE
> AND GONE
> HAD A GOOD TIME

In Aroostook County, Maine:

> HERE I LIE AND NO WONDER I'M DEAD,
> I FELL FROM A TREE AND HIT MY HEAD.

The epitaph in Scranton, Pennsylvania, declares:

IN MEMORY OF
ELLEN SHANNON
AGED 26 YEARS
WHO WAS FATALLY BURNED
MARCH 21ST 1870
BY THE EXPLOSION OF A LAMP
FILLED WITH "R. E. DANFORTH'S
NON-EXPLOSIVE
BURNING FLUID."

A man who fell from the roof of a house he was building was only twenty-seven years old at the time of his fatal accident. The flowery epitaph composed by his wife:

NINE FEET IN HEIGHT UPON A STAGE
ACTIVE IN HEALTH, IN BLOOM OF AGE.
BUT SUDDENLY THE STAGE GAVE WAY
HE FALLS AND DIES, HERE ENDS HIS DAY.

Political candidates and causes have also been the subject of last words.

On a Nebraska stone:

KIND FRIENDS I'VE
LEFT BEHIND
CAST YOUR VOTE FOR
WILLIAM JENNINGS BRYAN.

In a family plot in Minnesota:

NONE OF US EVER VOTED FOR
ROOSEVELT OR TRUMAN

A teetotaler's marker in Wyoming:

> FAITHFUL TO THE CAUSE OF PROHIBITION
> THEREFORE I MISSED PERDITION.

Two sprightly markers in Atlanta, Georgia read:

> BURIED WITH MY RIFLE.
> GOING TO SHOOT THE TAX COLLECTOR.

And that of a man who lost his property to urban development:

> GONE WITH THE WIND.

Earthly professions are often the subject of epitaphs. The marker over the grave of an Illinois doctor:

> I PRACTICED FOR OVER 50 YEARS
> AND NEVER LOST THAT MANY PATIENTS.

An Arkansas lawyer:

> WILLIAM HUMPHREY
> OFFICE NOW UPSTAIRS

On the tomb of Silas W. Sanderson, a California Supreme Court judge:

> FINAL DECREE.

A North Carolina member of the bar, who apparently didn't think much of his colleagues:

> THE ONLY HONEST LAWYER I EVER KNEW.

Another lawyer, from Madison, Wisconsin:

THE DEFENSE RESTS

The daughter of railroad conductor Charles B. Gunn had these words put on his tombstone:

PAPA—DID YOU WIND YOUR WATCH?

A New York journalist:

COPY ALL IN

Chicago traveling salesman Thomas W. Campbell:

MY TRIP IS ENDED
SEND MY SAMPLES HOME

An Elkhart, Indiana, high-school principal:

SCHOOL IS OUT
TEACHER HAS GONE HOME

The epitaph of Al Shean, member of the famous vaudeville team of Gallager and Shean, says:

AL SHEAN
BELOVED FATHER
BORN MAY 12, 1868
I COULD HAVE LIVED LONGER
BUT NOW IT'S TOO LATE
ABSOLUTELY MR. GALLAGHER—POSITIVELY MR. SHEAN
AUGUST 12, 1949

Boot Hill in Tombstone, Arizona, was the graveyard where the saved and unsaved were buried under pipe iron crosses. The epitaphs from the town's wild and woolly days are both colorful and candid.

VAN HOUTEN, MURDERED, 1879

HE WAS BEATEN IN THE FACE WITH A STONE
UNTIL HE DIED. TROUBLE WAS OVER HIS MINING
CLAIM, WHICH HE HAD NOT RECORDED.

CHAS. HELM, SHOT 1882
SHOT BY WM. MC CAULEY. TWO HOT-TEMPERED
RANCHERS, WHO DISAGREED OVER THE BEST
WAY TO DRIVE CATTLE, FAST OR SLOW.

JAMES HICKEY, 1881
SHOT BY WM. CLAYBORNE
HE WAS SHOT IN THE LEFT TEMPLE BY CLAY-
BORNE FOR HIS OVER-INSISTENCE THAT THEY
DRINK TOGETHER.

JOS. WETSELL, KILLED 1882
HE WAS STONED TO DEATH BY APACHES. HIS
FRIENDS WERE NOT FAR AWAY, AND IT WAS
THOUGHT THE INDIANS WANTED TO AVOID AT-
TRACTING THEIR ATTENTION BY SHOOTING HIM.

MARGARITA, STABBED BY GOLD DOLLAR
TWO DANCE HALL GIRLS QUARRELING OVER A
MAN, AND GOLD DOLLAR WON.

DAN DOWD
RED SAMPLE
TEX HOWARD
DAN KELLEY
LEGALLY HANGED

GEORGE JOHNSON
HANGED BY MISTAKE

JOHN GILLESPIE, 1882
HE DIED INSTANTLY WHEN HE WAS SHOT IN THE
HEAD, THE HEART AND THE STOMACH.

KILLEEN. SHOT BY FRANK LESLIE
RESULT OF A DISAGREEMENT OVER KILLEEN'S
WIFE. LESLIE MARRIED THE WIDOW.

JOHNNIE WILSON. SHOT BY KING
TWO GUNMEN'S DISCUSSION OF THE FASTEST
WAY TO DRAW, ENDED HERE.

FOO KEE
HE OWNED A RESTAURANT AND DIED FROM PTO-
MAINE POISONING.

WM. BOBIER
HE AND HIS PARTNER DISAGREED OVER A COCK-
FIGHT WITH TRAGIC RESULTS.

HERE LIES
LESTER MOORE
FOUR SLUGS
FROM A -44
NO LES
NO MORE.

The Tombstone *Epitaph* was the local newspaper that covered the rip-roaring town for ninety-five years. Its most famous story covered the gunfight at the O.K. Corral. When the paper ceased publishing in February 1975 because of "financial pressures," the Los Angeles *Times* headlined its demise: EPITAPH GOES TO GREAT BIG CORRAL IN SKY.

Equally colorful are the last words on tombstones scattered in other graveyards of the Old West.

In Searchlight, Nevada, once a thriving mining town:

AS I WAS LEADING THE MARE TO DRINK,
SHE KICKED AND KILLED ME QUICKER'N A WINK.

In Dodge City, Kansas:

HERE LAYS BUTCH,
WE PLANTED HIM RAW.
HE WAS QUICK ON THE TRIGGER
BUT SLOW ON THE DRAW.

The tough gold-mining camp of Leadville, Colorado, has two surviving stones that read:

AMOS RUTLEDGE HANGED HIMSELF.
WE WOULD HAVE DONE IT FOR HIM.

And:

UNDERNEATH THIS STONE IN ETERNAL REST
SLEEPS THE WILDEST ONE OF THE WAYWARD WEST
HE WAS A GAMBLER AND SPORT AND COWBOY TOO
AND HE LED THE PACE IN AN OUTLAW CREW
HE WAS SURE ON THE TRIGGER AND STAID TO THE END
BUT HE WAS NEVER KNOWN TO QUIT ON A FRIEND
IN THE RELATIONS OF DEATH ALL MEN ARE ALIKE
BUT IN LIFE THERE WAS ONLY ONE GEORGE W. PIKE

In nearby Cripple Creek, Colorado is this engraving above an unidentified miner:

HE CALLED
BILLY SMITH
A LIAR.

In a churchyard near Lincoln, Nebraska is a stone that can be read two ways:

ACCIDENTLY SHOT
AS A MARK OF AFFECTION
FROM HIS BROTHER.

In the same churchyard:

NOW AIN'T THIS TOO BAD.

Bon mot epitaphs survive elsewhere.
In Salt Lake City, Utah:

REJOICE!
SHE SLEEPS ALONE AT LAST.

John Gay's good-bye in a Malden, Massachusetts, cemetery:

LIFE IS A JEST, AND ALL THINGS SHOW IT.
I THOUGHT SO ONCE, AND NOW I KNOW IT.

In San Diego, California:

HE LIVED
HE DIED
HE CHOKED
HE CROAKED.

A New Orleans man left this final observation:

THIS IS WHAT I EXPECTED
BUT NOT SO SOON.

An unforgiving wife in Phoenix, Arizona, placed these words on her departed husband's stone:

THE OLD NUISANCE

The last words of a departed soul in Helena, Montana:

ANYTHING FOR A CHANGE.

Cedar Rapids, Iowa, has this farmer's stone:

> IN MEMORY OF JOHN F. TOTTEN
> GONE BUT NOT FORGOTTEN.

In Bloomington, Indiana:

> HERE LIES JOSIAH ROYCE
> I WOULD HAVE STAYED
> BUT I HAD NO CHOICE.

Well-known writers and entertainers have penned their own epitaphs. W. C. Fields:

> ALL THINGS CONSIDERED, I'D RATHER BE IN PHILADELPHIA.

Dorothy Parker:

> EXCUSE MY DUST.

An unrepentant actor:

> HERE LIES MICHAEL ARLEN, AS USUAL.

Perhaps the most gifted playwright in Broadway history:

> HERE LIES GEORGE S. KAUFMAN
> OVER MY DEAD BODY.

John Barrymore:

> SEE? I TOLD YOU I WAS SICK.

Two final notes concerning the plight of the departed are worthy of mention.

A Pittsburgh newspaper once carried this advertisement: "For sale, second-hand tombstone. Excellent buy for someone named Murphy."

In Los Angeles, a large cemetery announced that it was raising its prices for burial. A spokesman explained: "The reason is due to the increased cost of living."

12
ALL GOD'S CHILDREN

The rich vein of ecumenical humor crosses denominations and countries. The lure of interdenominational storytelling is apparently irresistible among clergymen and laymen of whatever rank and of whatever religious conviction. Such has been the case since the time of the Bible. And today, perhaps more than doctrine in many instances, humor is the tie that binds people of all faiths one to another. The following are offered in that spirit.

Despite their tragic and bloody history, the Irish have never wanted for humor. No matter how grim the circumstances, there has invariably been a moment for comic relief.

The story is still told in Ireland of the 1847 famine, when the only food available was parceled out by the churches. The food had been donated by non-Catholic Christians in England.

A grateful woman recipient of the rations asked her priest, "Did it ever occur to you, Father, that if it wasn't for the famine we'd be starving altogether?"

Even the current civil war in Ireland has bred an occasional smile.

An American reporter, freshly arrived in Belfast to cover the hostilities, asked a passerby, "What does a man do around here if he's an atheist?"

"Well now, son, that all depends on whether he's a Protestant atheist or a Catholic atheist."

Says Bishop Fulton J. Sheen: "The reason the Irish fight so often among themselves is that they're always assured of a worthy opponent."

Long before he was elected Lord Mayor of Dublin, Robert Briscoe, who is Jewish, helped Irish insurgents fight the British.

One day a strategy meeting was called in a church, and Briscoe was asked to remain outside and act as lookout.

The Irish leader explained: "You stand out here and watch for the British. That's easier than my having to explain to the priest what you're doing inside the church."

During Mayor Briscoe's regime, a new synagogue was built in Dublin. Since Ireland's population is 95 percent Catholic, the Irish were briefly stymied as to what the temple should be called. But for tourists who wished to visit the house of worship, it was soon designated by cabbies as "the new Protestant synagogue."

A favorite toast in Ireland among Catholics and Protestants: "May you be in heaven thirty minutes before the devil knows you're dead."

Thunder rumbled and lightning flashed. It was the worst storm of the year and heavy rain had slickened the highway outside Dublin, causing a truck barreling down the road to skid and overturn.

The driver, near death, was pinned under a wheel.

"Get me a rabbi," he told the first policeman who reached the scene.

"Are you of the faith?" the policeman asked.

"Oh, yes."

"Then why would a fine Irish Catholic be wanting a rabbi?"

"Sure, and you wouldn't think of asking a priest to come out on a night like this!"

Then there was the Irish Catholic who said he would rather die than be buried in a Protestant cemetery.

The Englishman, back in London after a vacation in Ireland, told a friend he'd been surprised to see churches of virtually every denomination besides Catholic.

"I suppose the Irish build all those non-Catholic churches because they believe in freedom of religion," his friend said.

"No," replied the Englishman, "they build them for spite."

A popular limerick in Ireland:

> A girl from Belfast name of Alice,
> Drew rude things on the Vatican Palace.
> She said, "Now this deed,
> Comes from aesthetic need,
> And not from a Protestant malice."

After a trip abroad, the Irish Catholic matron confronted the Protestant customs man.

"What have we here?" the customs man asked suspiciously, holding up a large bottle.

"'Tis water from Lourdes I'm bringing home with me."

He opened the bottle and tasted the contents.

"This isn't water. It's French brandy."

"Sure, then," she said, "it's a miracle!"

The nun's car sputtered to a halt, and she walked to a filling station. The proprietor gave her enough gas to get her vehicle started in the only container he had available—a beer bottle.

As she was pouring the contents from the beer bottle into her tank, a gentleman of Protestant persuasion pulled up beside her and watched in amazement.

"Sister," he said, "we may have our differences, but I certainly admire your faith."

When President John F. Kennedy visited Ireland he was awarded honorary degrees by both Trinity College, which is Catholic, and National College, a Protestant seat of higher learning.

Asked which team he would root for when the two schools played their annual rugby game, President Kennedy replied diplomatically: "I'll cheer for Trinity and pray for National."

Movie and television star Pat O'Brien regales audiences in his nightclub act with the story of the Notre Dame football player who went to confession.

"Father, I kicked an opposing player in the shins."

"May God forgive you," the priest said.

"Then I stepped on another player's hand with my cleats."

"Terrible. Terrible."

"And then I socked another player in the mouth and knocked out six of his teeth."

The priest was in a rage. "You've disgraced the fine name of Notre Dame by playing dirty against the opposing team. By the way, what school were you playing?"

"Southern Methodist."

"Oh, well," said the priest, "boys will be boys."

Like the Irish, the Jews have lightened their burdens with humor.

Prime Minister Golda Meir once said, "The Bible tells us that Moses wandered through the desert for forty years before he found a home for our people. Tell me, why did he have to settle on such a controversial site?"

The Jewish politician in Tel Aviv told his friend, "I blame all our troubles on Moses."

"Why?"

"When Moses crossed the Red Sea, if he'd made a left turn instead of a right, the Arabs would've gotten the sand and we would have gotten the oil."

A rabbi was complaining to a colleague, "Some members of my congregation have become Quakers."

"That's too bad."

"It's gotten so that some of my best Jews are Friends."

Perhaps the most common name in Arab nations is Ali. After a movie fan in Lebanon saw Ali McGraw in *Love Story,* she said to her husband, "I didn't realize she was a Moslem."

One American representative to the United Nations said of the Palestinian problem: "Jews and Arabs should solve their disagreements in a truly Christian spirit."

Visiting the Vatican's Sistine Chapel, a group of Baptist tourists were informed by their guide, "It took four years to paint the ceiling."

Sighed one woman, "They must have the same landlord I do."

Terence Cardinal Cooke was given a ticket to the show *Jesus Christ, Superstar* by a Protestant friend.

Afterwards, the cardinal was asked by his friend, "What did you think of it?"

"It's not as good as the Book."

The conversation between the rabbi, the minister, and the priest turned to how each denomination celebrated Christmas morning.

The minister and priest explained that Protestants and Catholics give thanks for God's bounty and blessings and on Christmas morning they open their presents.

"We do it a little differently," the rabbi said. "On Christmas morning my entire family goes to my brother's department store. We look at the empty shelves, and then we all join in singing 'What a Friend We Have in Jesus.' "

A minister, a priest, and a rabbi went fishing. They rented a rowboat and paddled out about a half-mile from shore. Shortly, they ran out of bait.

The minister got out of the boat and walked on top of the water to shore, bought some bait, and came back.

The rabbi, observing this, was astonished.

An hour later the three clergymen were hungry. So the priest left the boat, walked on the water, and returned with sandwiches.

Again, the rabbi was astonished.

The rabbi decided that if the minister and priest could walk on water, he could, too. He stepped into the water and promptly sank. The minister and the priest quickly dragged him back into the boat.

The rabbi, however, was not to be outdone. He tried walking on the water three times, and each time he failed.

Finally, smiling, the minister said to the priest, "Before he drowns, shall we tell him where the rocks are?"

The Methodist church welcomed a new member to its flock.

Asked to tell the congregation some of his background, the man said, "I come from the Deep South. And if you ain't a Baptist down there, then someone has been messing with your religion."

The little Catholic boy and the little Jewish boy were talking about religion.

The Catholic boy said, "My priest knows more than your rabbi."

"Why shouldn't he?" the Jewish lad said. "You tell him everything."

Art Linkletter, whose father was a lay Baptist preacher, was interviewing a seven-year-old girl who attended a Catholic school.

"Does your mother do anything to make your father mad?"

"Yes."

"What?"

"She cooks the wrong kind of fish on Friday."

"What kind is the wrong kind?"

"Pork chops."

The atheist housewife went to a fundamentalist Protestant church and listened to the pastor preach on the end of the world and the Second Coming.

The sermon made a believer out of her and she ran home and began cleaning.

Her husband asked, "Why of all days are you cleaning the house on Sunday?"

"My goodness," she said, "the world's going to end and the Lord's coming back. I wouldn't want Him to find the place in a mess."

The Baptist minister was looking at used cars. One struck his eye and he asked the salesman, who was Catholic, if it was a good buy.

"Yes and no."

"I don't understand."

"She runs—but, Reverend, I don't think you have the vocabulary to make her run."

"I'm engaged to an Irish boy," the Protestant girl breathlessly told her mother after coming home from a date.

"Oh, really!"

"No, O'Reilly."

One hundred men were employed in the factory. Ninety-seven were Protestant, three Catholic.

One Protestant and one Catholic ran for president of the factory union.

The Protestant won by a vote of 97-3.

Congratulating him, the Catholic said, "You guys really stick together, don't you?"

The priest and the rabbi were discussing the potential of promotion in the Catholic church.

"If he's capable, works hard and prays hard, a priest can eventually become a bishop and perhaps a cardinal," the Catholic clergyman explained.

"Is that as far as he can go?" the rabbi asked.

"No, there are a few men who are so exceptional that we elect them popes."

"And that's as far as a priest can go?"

"Yes. After all, he can't become Jesus Christ."

The rabbi thought a minute and smiled. "Why not? One of our boys did it."

In the course of a conversation about the differences in their religions, the minister said to the priest, "We're not really far apart. We both preach the same Gospel."

"That's true," said the priest, "you in your way, and I in His."

The late NBC newscaster Frank McGee was flawlessly broadcasting the details of Pope Paul VI's visit to Yankee Stadium in New York City. Then McGee explained to the millions who were listening why he was asking his colleague to take over.

"I'm not Catholic and, therefore, not too familiar with the rituals you are about to see. So I'm going to turn the microphone over to Irving R. Levine—who spent many years in Rome."

In a small Midwest town, the Methodist and Presbyterian churches decided to hold joint services during the summer.

All went well, except that each denomination used a slightly different version of the Lord's Prayer.

At the end of the summer, both congregations went back to their own churches, with the ministers issuing a joint announcement: "The time has now come for the Methodists to return to their trespasses and leave the Presbyterians to their debtors."

"Which denomination do you prefer?" the zealous Baptist asked a man to whom he was witnessing.

"It don't matter much—either tens or twenties."

The priest and the rabbi were sitting ringside at a prizefight.

Just before the bout was to get underway, one of the boxers knelt and blessed himself.

The rabbi asked, "Father, does that help?"

"Not a bit if he can't fight."

The Baptist workman repairing a hole in the roof of a Catholic church was a bit of a practical joker.

Peering through the hole, he could see an elderly woman praying. The roofer said, "This is Jesus. Your prayers are being answered."

Unimpressed, the woman kept praying.

Again the man said, "This is Jesus. Your prayers are being answered."

Whereupon, the woman said, "Please be quiet. I'm talking to Your mother."

The priest invited his minister friend to his apartment for a cup of tea.

"Father," the minister exclaimed, "you have such comfortable quarters here, so much better than mine. I must say I envy you."

"Well," said the priest, "you ministers have your better halves and we priests have our better quarters."

The Jewish lady and her Protestant friend went shopping for the holidays.

As they said good-bye after several hours in the department store, the lady of Jewish extraction said: "If I don't see you before Christmas —have a Merry Hanukkah."

The Jewish man was praying to God in the temple.
"What's troubling you?" he heard a voice ask.
"My son has left the Jewish faith and become a Christian."
"Yours, too?"

The lovely but flighty lady found herself sitting between a minister and a rabbi at a dinner party.
She said, "I feel as if I were a leaf between the Old and the New Testament."
Winking, the rabbi said, "That page, Madam, is usually a blank."

The final ecumenical word is perhaps best left to the nine-year-old girl who'd just moved into the neighborhood and struck up a friendship with a small boy next door.
"I'm a Methodist," the boy said. "What church do you go to?"
"I don't go to a church. I go to a temple. I'm Jewish "
"What's that?"
The girl explained: "There are Protestants, Catholics, and Jews, but they're all just different ways of voting for God."